"Michele Howe's newest book
advice on how to be a *grand*,
of her delightful books, she includes heartwarming stories and spiritual
guidance designed to help the reader take the next step forward toward
becoming something better than they were before reading the book. I
can't recommend this encouraging resource enough!"

—**Rick Johnson, best-selling author,**
10 Things Great Dads Do: Strategies for Raising Great Kids
and *Overcoming Toxic Parenting:*
How to Be a Good Parent When Yours Wasn't

"A wise and welcome companion through the seasons of life, Michele
Howe helped me navigate the transition from parent to parent of adult
children. Now I'm an over-the-moon, thrilled member of the grandparent club. *There's a Reason They Call It* Grand*parenting* celebrates the
profound sacredness of supporting adult children, and treating grandchildren with dignity and respect. As image-bearers of our loving God,
grandparents provide unconditional acceptance, open arms, and grace
upon grace. Michele offers clarity, joy, and appreciation for the vital and
life-giving position of grandparents in God's family tree."

—**PeggySue Wells, best-selling author**
Coauthor, *Bonding with Your Child through Boundaries*,
Slavery in the Land of the Free, **and**
Rediscovering Your Happily Ever After

"You're probably looking at this book because you want to be the *best*
grandparent possible. In *There's a Reason They Call It* Grand*parenting*,
Michele Howe does a masterful job of covering the fun part, the challenging part, and the necessary part of carrying out this role in a God-
honoring way that will bless the children of your own sons and daughters.
You'll discover important take-away truths, powerful ways to pray for your
grandchildren, and action steps that will give you the momentum and
wisdom to be a transformational influence in the lives of these precious
members of your family."

—**Carol Kent, national speaker and author**
He Holds My Hand: Experiencing God's Presence & Protection

"Every grandparent who wants to be an *awesome* grandparent *needs* a copy of this book. As the title suggests, each chapter deftly describes what that looks like, why it's important, and how to become not just a grandparent, but a *grand*parent. Michele Howe offers here a deep and meaningful guide chock-full of real-life, accessible examples for anyone wishing to fully embrace the role of grandparent. Henceforth, this book shall be my go-to gift for new grandparents."

—**Rhonda Owens, coauthor,**
Undivided Family: Living for & Not Just with One and Another
and *Undivided Marriage: When TWO People Become ONE Flesh*

MICHELE HOWE

There's a Reason They Call It
GRAND
parenting

MICHELE HOWE

There's a Reason They Call It
GRAND
parenting

HENDRICKSON
PUBLISHERS

There's a Reason They Call It *Grand*parenting

© 2017 Hendrickson Publishers Marketing, LLC
P. O. Box 3473
Peabody, Massachusetts 01961-3473
www.hendrickson.com

ISBN 978-1-68307-035-1

Scripture quotations contained herein are taken from the Holy Bible, New International Version®, NIV®. Copyright © 1973, 1978, 1984, 2011 by Biblica, Inc.™ Used by permission of Zondervan. All rights reserved worldwide. www.zondervan.com The "NIV" and "New International Version" are trademarks registered in the United States Patent and Trademark Office by Biblica, Inc.™

Printed in the United States of America

First Printing—November 2017

Library of Congress Cataloging-in-Publication Data

A catalog record for this title is available from the Library of Congress
Hendrickson Publishers Marketing, LLC ISBN 978-1-68307-035-1

To my beloved grandchildren:

Logan James Zatko
Tyler William Zatko
Jonathan Dale Zatko
&
Charis Myra Canning

Contents

Acknowledgements

Working with the fabulous Hendrickson team is becoming something of a habit these past few years—a life-enriching habit I hope never ceases. As an author, I have an increasingly greater appreciation for everything my publishing team does to create the book you now hold in your hands. I am ever grateful for how easy my editors, Patricia Anders and Maggie Swofford, make it for me to write. Their keen eyes catch all my mistakes (and mind you, there are quite a few of them). These skilled professionals possess terrific ability to know what works (as opposed to what doesn't), which makes my book far more valuable, enriching, and applicable to the everyday life of my readers. Thank you, Patricia and Maggie. You are editors extraordinaire and I appreciate everything you do!

My sincerest thanks goes also to Meg Rusick and Maggie Swofford who get the word out (and keep my work in the public's eye) with singular skill and finesse. I also want to say a supersized thank you to Tina Donohue for the lovely cover design and to Phil Frank for the typesetting of this book. Please accept this author's humble thanks for all of your steady (and stellar) work.

And a final thanks to my agent, Les Stobbe, for steering this little ship of mine to the right publisher at the right time. You have helped me stay afloat these many years in the often turbulent waters of publishing.

Introduction

When I was a young teen, I remember sitting on the back porch of our home reading a magazine in the brilliant summer sunshine and thinking to myself that I could do this too (a rather daring thought for a teenager). "This" meaning I could write an article and get it published in a real honest-to-goodness print magazine. Then I set my magazine aside and promptly forgot that little notion for many long years. It wasn't until after I married in my early twenties and started a family of my own that I began to revisit my long-forgotten dream to write articles or, well, anything for publication.

As a stay-at-home mom, I rediscovered my love for the written word—both reading and writing it. Within eighteen months of the birth of my first child, I sold my very first article, and I haven't stopped writing for the past thirty-two years. My "body of work" includes book reviewing, author interviews, single-parenting guides, parenting articles, nonfiction pieces on health and well-being, children's ice-breaker games, adult devotionals, and Bible curricula. I even wrote a few fictional stories. Those several thousand articles prepared me to write books. At last count, I'm working on book number eighteen and still loving every minute of the process.

1

In the same way that long years of article writing prepared the way to book writing, I believe my parenting years paved the way to grandparenting. Real-life experiences always build, grow, and continue to shape and form the people we are today. First, I became a mother of four children. Today, I am the grandmother of four grandchildren (and counting!). What I learned along the way (as a result of making mistakes, enduring failures, and overcoming frustrations) I now utilize to make myself a better grandmother than I was a mother.

One of the primary themes of this text readers will continually revisit is the life-altering distinction between being a mere grandparent and choosing to be a *grand*parent. I hope you'll choose the latter—every time. Becoming a *grand*parent is living with eternity in mind—all the time. It means going the extra mile (or more, many more) for the sake of your grandchildren. It will entail sacrifice of every sort. Time. Money. Energy. Sleep. But every sort of giving up and giving away the best of what we have and are is all good. . . in the light of eternity.

*Grand*parenting is all about bending the knee before our Lord Jesus Christ and asking him for our marching orders. Then we get up from our knees and get busy loving our grandchildren in ways they will remember, value, and appreciate. *Grand*parenting takes every bit of our parenting experience and sifts out what didn't work the first time around with our children to glean only the finest insights, wisdom, perceptiveness, and giftedness we have to offer our grandchildren. Catch the vision of growing into the kind of *grand*parent who can impact the entire next generation for Christ. It's for the good of your grandchildren, and it will do you good.

Part One
What Is Grandparenting?

Chapter 1

The Difference between a Grandparent and a Grandparent

His divine power has given us everything we need
for a godly life through our knowledge of him who
called us by his own glory and goodness. . . . For this
reason, make every effort to add to your faith goodness;
and to goodness, knowledge; and to knowledge,
self-control; and to self-control, perseverance; and
to perseverance, godliness; and to godliness, mutual
affection; and to mutual affection, love. For if you
possess these qualities in increasing measure, they
will keep you from being ineffective and unproductive
in your knowledge of our Lord Jesus Christ.

2 Peter 1:3, 5–8

*Wise, mature, godly people live aware of the spiritual;
they see it in every situation of life. They see the
spiritual implications in everything they do, in every
situation they are in. This is what we must aim to
produce in our (children and grandchildren). To
do this we must be spiritually minded ourselves.*

Paul Tripp

5

I'm convinced that one of the finest seasons of life is when your children have grown and gone (but not too far away). Then comes that eventful day when one of your adult kids looks you straight in the eye and announces he/she is going to be a parent. It is one of those starry-eyed conversations when you can't get the questions bubbling up in your mind and out of your mouth fast enough. When? Where? How? (Well, maybe not how.)

I still remember sitting in the passenger seat driving to a nearby city with my eldest daughter when she told me she was expecting their first baby. Oh my. Emotions flooded through my heart and soul. I suddenly started imagining all sorts of lovely pink and blue scenarios in my mind. You know the kind. Me cuddling a rosy-faced infant in front of firelight. Me pushing a chortling toddler higher and higher on a swing at the playground. Me teaching an elementary aged youngster how to bake cookies, cinnamon rolls, and more. Me taking a teenager to the mall for a special lunch and some one-on-one shopping. My mind raced ahead through the years while thoughts of sugarplums danced through my head. Until they didn't.

A few days after my daughter made her grand announcement I felt anything but happy. I felt scared. I suddenly began reliving all the years of sleepless nights when our four children were infants and we would have done just about anything for a long stretch of sleep. I recalled those seasons of sickness when one illness would spread from one child to four and then my husband and I would catch it on the rebound. Memories of school worries, school bullies, school crushes, and school work all tumbled through my overactive brain. I, merely the grandmother to be, wasn't all that sure that I could go through the trials and tribulations of parent-hood even from a sidelines position. Then God reminded me that he is the giver of life, the sustainer of life, and the one who carefully guards each life. Oh, blessed relief.

What a divine assurance I felt when I realized that what-ever part we were to play in our future grandchildren's lives, God would be right there with us, guiding our steps, giving us wisdom, lending us his knowledge and understanding as we sought to support our adult children in the lifelong task of parenting. Amen and amen.

As the title of this chapter suggests, the difference be-tween a *grand*parent and grandparent is, well, immense. A *grand*parent seeks to pack a positive punch of biblical influence into their grandchildren's lives. They prayer-fully seek out the most effective ways to lend a hand to their adult children in both practical and fun ways. They don't simply seek to spoil their grandchildren with good times or material extras—rather, they realize, as Paul Tripp states above, that all of life is spiritual in nature. The wise *grand*parent will do everything they can to demonstrate and illustrate the love of Jesus Christ to their grandchildren. They begin by investing in prayer before the little one even enters the world. *Grand*parents, as opposed to grandparents who are in name only that next generation of relatives, un-derstand how fleeting life is and proactively look for divine opportunities to point their grandchildren to Jesus.

No matter what the circumstances, *grand*parents make the most of every day to pray, petition, and put their grandchildren's welfare near the top of their priorities. Grandchildren are the next generation of believers (or they can be) only if *grand*parents and parents love them to the Lord, instruct their tender hearts in the way of life, and give sacrificially for their behalf. *Grand*parenting is a high and holy calling. Amen and amen.

𝒫ℰ *Take-away Action Thought*

I will seek the Lord for better understanding on the role he wants me to take in *grand*parenting my grandchildren. Then, I will take practical steps to bring this visionary role into daily reality.

My Heart's Cry to You, O Lord

Help me, Father, to go first to you as I seek the best ways to invest in the lives of my grandchildren. Give me an eternal perspective that supersedes everything else. I want to love my grandchildren in ways that will demonstrate your perfect love, but I cannot do this in my own strength. My grandchildren need the light of your Holy Spirit to guide them, just as I do. Help me discipline myself to pray daily for them, to intercede hour by hour as you bring them to my mind, and to point them to you continually. Our world is a battlefield, Lord, and I know it well. Give me everything I require to bring spiritual protection, practical provision, and emotional encouragement to my grandchildren. Teach me how to speak life into their tender hearts—and never stop. Amen.

Grand Ideas

1. Begin a journal just for your grandchildren. Write your prayer requests on its empty pages, and then watch and see how God faithfully answers.

2. Talk to other grandparents about ways they have found are successful in offering spiritual instruction to their grandchildren.

3. Pray big for your grandchildren. Ask God to bring each one to a saving faith in Jesus Christ at an early age.

Chapter 2

It Takes Someone Special to Be a Grandparent

For we are God's handiwork, created in Christ Jesus to do good works, which God prepared in advance for us to do.

Ephesians 2:10

"Grand: Striking in size, scope, extent, or conception; very good, wonderful."

Merriam-Webster

As much as I would love for my adult children and my grandchildren to describe me using some of the adjectives above ("very good," "wonderful"), I'd be far more excited if I knew I was fully actualizing the "striking scope, extent, or conception" aspects of being a *grand*parent who truly gets the largess of potential we have as the next generation's influencers for good. Being a grandparent means so much more than merely buying holiday gifts, sending birthday presents, and occasionally showing up for a Little League game (when the weather is practically perfect). Rather, true *grand*parenting entails embracing the vision God lays out in his word that every single one of us has been singled out and prepared in advance to do good things by God's grace alone.

Exciting, isn't it? To know that the Creator God has chosen us before time to be part of his big plan to help spread the good news. And what better objects to bestow this eternal change-maker message than with our own family? Sure, we all remember those grim moments of parental failure. We can bring to mind painful conversations we had with our now adult children when we blew it in major proportions. We can rehearse until the end of time those seasons when, although we wanted to catch a fresh vision for parenting, we struggled instead just to get out of bed in the morning because we were so weary.

What I love most about the prospect of growing into a *grand*parent who truly gets the stakes of influencing our next generation is this: God can (and will) use every mistake, every mishap, and every parental fail I experienced to equip me to do it better this time around. In simple terms, I'm not as tired as I was when I was parenting 24/7. Today, I'm older (hopefully wiser) and, given the previous two claims, I've got loads more perspective. The eternal kind. The kind of perspective that lasts and sees past the often discouraging daily realities parents face. Hallelujah to graduating from parent to *grand*parent!

How large is your scope? How often do you quietly consider your God-given calling to encourage and reach out to your adult children as they parent their own children?

Have we as grandparents forgotten the weight of parenting infants to toddlers to elementary to high school and beyond? Have we instead chosen to do "our own thing" with "our own time" and "our own money" now that our adult children have moved out? What must God think of parents who taught their children to think of others first and to be mindful of serving the least of these, but who are now turning their backs on their children's and grandchildren's needs? How sad, shameful, and so utterly short-sighted.

Our society names it and claims it that if you're a parent of an adult child, you are now free to live out your wildest dreams and desires in excess, no matter how your choices may affect others. We have forgotten that the Bible never speaks of "retirement"—that entity is a purely cultural animal. What we need to bring to mind is the principle found in Ephesians 2:10 where we are told that even before we were born, God had planned for us to do good things. Let's take him at his word and trust him to equip us for all the good he has planned. And let us begin by giving thanks to God for allowing us the privilege of being part of his big plan of redemption.

Take-away Action Thought

When I start to doubt the potential impact I can have on my grandchildren, I will immediately stop these negative thoughts and go to God's word to give me the eternal perspective I need.

My Heart's Cry to You, O Lord

Help me to spend time in your presence daily, Lord, quietly seeking what you would have me do to help my grandchildren know who you are. I want to be on the job and ready all the time, not just when I feel like it or when I have free time. Give me the needed push I require to stay diligently involved and actively interceding for this next generation. Never allow me to grow selfish with my time and resources. Rather, show me exactly how you want me to funnel my blessings into the lives of those around me. I fully believe that you bless me so I can be a blessing to others. Help me to never forget that powerful truth. Amen.

Grand Ideas

1. Brainstorm with seasoned grandparents, and ask them what they believe has made the most lasting impact on their grandchildren.
2. Ask your adult children to keep you in the loop on what they see as their children's most pressing spiritual needs.
3. Talk with God weekly about your role in helping to form your grandchildren's lives. Always be open to the Holy Spirit's conviction.

 *Chapter 3*

It All Begins with Prayer

Pray continually, give thanks in all circumstances;
for this is God's will for you in Christ Jesus.
1 Thessalonians 5:17–18

Prayer does not equip us for greater work—
prayer is the greater work.
Oswald Chambers

I remember being the mom of four children under the age of six and feeling guilty because I just couldn't seem to find a regular alone time with the Lord. Sure, I knew he was always with me throughout the day, but I longed to be alone in silence, away from the voices of my children so that I could calm all those voices in my own head. I tried getting up early, but our alarm was already going off in the wee hours because my husband is a high school teacher. I creatively attempted to get all four of my children to nap simultaneously, but you can guess how often I succeeded. My last resort was to pray, read my Bible, and silently meditate on his goodness right before I went to bed. Ahem. I am a morning person through and through, so attempting a nightly quiet time was an epic fail. I was frustrated and just plain at a loss as to how to make my precious (and oh so needed) time with the Lord a daily occurrence. Finally, God in his mercy allowed me to hear someone else's voice besides my own perpetually sleep-deprived one. Enter an older, wiser, been-through-it-all, grandmotherly lady, who assured me that the Lord was already intimately aware of everything I needed to be a good wife, mother, friend, and whatever other role I had to fill. The problem wasn't that I had to wait until my kids had grown up before I could carve out some time with Jesus. Rather, I needed to begin looking at it differently. This wise woman recalled her own angst as a much younger woman who felt just like me: out of sorts and longing for more of him.

She challenged me to stop viewing time alone with Jesus as the primary way to communicate with him most effectively. She reminded me of the verse in 1 Thessalonians 5 in which we are commanded to "pray continually" and "give thanks for everything." This brief conversation ended with a key piece of advice: that I begin viewing prayer like breathing. Like breathing in, I needed to take in the truths found in Scripture by either memorizing them or writing them on cards and placing them in prominent positions around my home. Like breathing out, I needed to speak out my thoughts to God, aloud or silently, talking with him about everything: hopes, dreams, disappointments, fears, worries, and more. I needed to breathe in and out, all day long.

I did as my friend suggested. I started breathing in God's word whenever I was able to snatch a few minutes here and there, and then I started breathing out my prayers—all day long. This echoes the words above by Oswald Chambers: "Prayer doesn't prepare us for the greater work—prayer is the greater work."

Many years have passed since my own four children were running around my house all day (and night). Still, I find that the "In. . . Out. . ." practice I adopted all those years ago serves me well even today. Sure, I now have scheduled alone time for reading and praying. However, some of my best praying goes on while I'm busy cleaning, cooking, running errands, or settling down to work in my office. I've found that God has retrained my mind to be attentive to him all through the day. What began out of necessity years ago has now become so ingrained in my heart and mind that I gladly welcome the Holy Spirit's nudges to pray when he brings someone to my mind at any time, all the time.

As *grand*parents who understand that life requires constant conversation with the Lord, what better habit could we adopt than that of daily, hourly, minute-by-minute intercession on behalf of those we love? When we first hear the news of our adult child's upcoming baby, we should start praying for them and for their child. Then, after our grandchild has been welcomed into the world, we should create a journal of prayers for him or her. Year by year, our prayers should develop as they do. Each and every day, *grand*parents can go directly to God to get his prayer instructions, which will provide us with his truth all day long. But it all begins with prayer.

♫ Take-away Action Thought

I will set create a journal for my prayers for each grandchild, and I will happily make note of how God answers each prayer. I will purpose to pray continually, and I will give thanks in everything.

My Heart's Cry to You, O Lord

Father, help me discipline myself to spend time daily getting to know you better. Show me your glory, Lord, every time I open your word. Help me to pray faith-filled and grace-infused prayers for my family. Give me those nudges through the day and into the night when my family needs extra prayer support. Lord, help me to honor your command to pray continually. I want to live with a keen awareness of your constant presence in my life. Rather than worrying, I will pray away my concerns and keep my eyes focused on you. Amen.

Grand Ideas

1. Work into your daily quiet time specific prayers for each of your grandchildren such as asking the Lord to help each one come to saving faith in Christ and asking for the Holy Spirit to teach them truth all day and into the night hours.
2. As you go through the day, keep your prayer journal close at hand so you can easily jot down any prayer requests God brings to your mind.
3. When you are with your grandchildren, consistently take time to pray with and for them.

Chapter 4

It All Ends with Prayer

May the God of peace, who through the blood of
the eternal covenant brought back from the dead
our Lord Jesus, that great Shepherd of the sheep,
equip you with everything good for doing his will.

Hebrews 13:20–21

Love people. Know them. Speak truth into their lives.
Help them do what God has called them to do.

Paul Tripp

L ife is full of firsts and lasts (and everything in between). I'm reminded of that old saying that our life
is what lies between the dashes found on graveyard
tombstones. Living near a rather grand cemetery where
many of my husband's extended family is buried, I've no-
ticed the various headstones and the final words of tribute
paid to loved ones. Some are quite touching. Others, not
so much. Reading the tombstone headers, both good and
bad, brings me back to the necessity of living lives full of
vision and for eternal purpose. Just like those words etched

on the gravestones, individuals choose either to live for themselves or for something larger.

Whether we are newbies or gonna-bes to the wide world of grandparenting, I believe we would do well to live our days with Hebrews 13:20–21 in mind. These verses are a robust reminder that God—our great Shepherd, Savior, and King—truly has given us everything good for doing his will so we might do what is pleasing to him. Reading and meditating on the truth found in this verse, I believe, sums up the great commandment to love one's neighbor as oneself. What better way to impact the next generation (our grandchildren among them) than by loving, knowing, and speaking God's truth into people's lives, helping them achieve what God has planned for them. It's a two-for-one, win-win proposition. A win-win for us as the Christ followers engaged in battling for the hearts of our grandchildren. A win-win for those we're investing our lives in as we help equip our grandchildren to run their own particular races well.

Getting back to the basics of praying before running interference (unwanted interfere at that!) on behalf of our grandchildren, it is critical to remember the hard truth that sometimes God and our adult children say no. I wonder if grandparents would hear fewer no's from God and our adult children if we took the time to ask the Lord what he wants of us as circumstances arise. *Grand*parents need to accept the fact that sometimes our grand plans "end with prayer" simply because we're attempting to meet a need

God doesn't want us to tackle. After receiving so many no's, hearing a yes from God (or our adult children) forces *grand*parents to pose some practical questions: How do I love them? How do I go about knowing them? How do I speak truth into their lives? How do I help prepare them for facing life in general? To get those answers, the only solution is to pray. Before we take even one step out our back door, we need to quiet ourselves before the Lord and ask him to give us our marching orders for the day. I wonder how often I miss God's plans for me because I roll right into action before even asking him if he wants me to get involved.

Let's be honest: There are many moments when we see a need in our grandchildren's lives (as we did all those years ago in our now adult children's lives), and we jump into the situation without praying first. We long to bring a smile to our grandchildren's faces by buying them something they want. We feel happy when we meet a need. We anticipate fun-filled visits when we can pile on the goodies (food, festive activities, and frivolous extras). God, the greatest parent, knows exactly what our little ones need most. Their parents, too, know better than we grandparents what is most needed for their growth.

In all seasons of life, let us wise *grand*parents first quiet our hearts and minds in God's presence before leaping into the situation headlong. Then, and only then, should we carefully wade in with our thoughts, suggestions, or offers to supply something. From beginning to end, prayer must supersede involvement, including the loving involvement of the *grand*est of *grand*parents.

21

✄ *Take-away Action Thought*

When I feel the temptation to jump in headlong to meet a need in my grandchild's life, I will stop first and take the needed time to pray and seek God's will in the matter.

My Heart's Cry to You, O Lord

Father, help me to seek you before I leap into action in regard to my grandchildren's lives. You know what a temptation it is for me to want to take away pain and suffering. But you also know that we all learn the most, grow the deepest, and are molded into your image when we have to endure hardship. I never want to short-circuit the good you are doing in my grandchildren's lives by giving them too much too often. Help me take time to sit quietly in your presence and seek your will before offering my help. I want them to grow into mature, loving, selfless adults who mirror Jesus in thought, word, and deed. Give me your wisdom to understand best how to love them. Amen.

Grand Ideas

1. When you see a need you want to meet in your grandchildren's lives, consult the Lord first and then seek your adult children's permission.
2. Learn how to prayerfully develop self-control and view your grandchildren's learning experiences as opportunities for character growth.
3. In all things, seek to meet needs, offer support, and give materially in a balanced manner.

Chapter 5

Hospitality Is Spelled "Grandparents"

Offer hospitality to one another without grumbling.
. . . If anyone serves, he should do so with the
strength God provides, so that in all things
God may be praised through Jesus Christ.

1 Peter 4:9, 11

*You can become the kind of person you've always
wanted to be around. The kind of person who makes
the Jesus and His gospel winsome to all who come
within the reach of your grateful, "happy spirit."*

Nancy Leigh DeMoss

*T*he older I get, the more I treasure a good night's sleep. There are some brutally long sleepless nights when I would literally pay to sleep straight through to the morning alarm. Between my intermittent hot flashes (with the accompanying pounding heart palpitations) and my husband's CPAP machine's whooshing and humming, I frequently feel like I'm in the middle of some humid, howling thunderstorm. Try as I might, I just can't get away from the semiconscious distractions (or get back to sleep). Unfortunately for me, I know for sure that I will not sleep more soundly when my grandchildren come for a visit. With three little people under my roof, I revert back to a motherly light-sleeping, always-on-the-alert mode. As a result, I simply don't sleep well. I hear every small bump in the night and almost anxiously wait to be awakened by some small voice tugging at my hand or whispering in my ear.

That said, even though I try to do all that I can to be prepared for my grandchildren's (and their parents') visits, there are times when all the cooking, cleaning, and even resting isn't possible. I know I'm going into my caregiving stint somewhat compromised, but I have no choice. I can, however, choose my attitude. I can let go of my desire to be super organized with meals prepped and ready to be cooked or served; fresh, clean sheets on every bed; and a house that sparkles as though Mr. Clean has just paid a visit. I can, in fact, internalize that winsome, grateful "happy spirit" that Nancy Leigh DeMoss writes about. Yes, that's what is needed most when I'm hosting family, friends, and others in my home. Above all, I need to remind myself of what is most important in life. Here's a hint: It isn't what folks see when they enter in; it's how I make them feel. I hope that when guests enter my home, they feel welcomed, loved, accepted, and treasured.

Pruning away a sinful attitude is hard work. Yet I fear that I give more attention to the aspects of my life that I can see, such as the house, the food, the gifts, and the whole external picture. In the end, those are trifling matters in comparison to offering what matters more than anything else to our loved ones—our heart. Our grandchildren want to be welcomed into our loving arms when they come over, not into a house that's merely outwardly beautiful. They hunger for unconditional love, total acceptance, and lots of warm, generous expressions of our appreciation for each of them.

It is tragic that some grandparents neglect hospitality because they feel their house is too small, their budget is too tight, or they don't have the energy for noisy miniature guests. But let's be honest with ourselves: we all face occasional (or continual) constraints of less than perfect houses, tight food budgets, and limited energy resources. We need to remember that God promises to provide the strength we need to be hospitable. He blesses us with all that we need so that we can, in turn, bless others. We can't let ourselves pass up opportunities to be hospitable just because we're not in the mood or are uncomfortable. What we can offer is always enough. Let's get busy finding new and creative ways to be hospitable.

Take-away Action Thought

I will not use excuses to neglect offering hospitality to my loved ones. Instead, I will reach for my calendar and set up three different dates to open my home to others in the near future.

25

My Heart's Cry to You, O Lord

Help me, Father, to be keenly aware of how much you have given me materially, relationally, emotionally, and spiritually. According to your word, I have everything I need to be hospitable toward others. Everything. You understand that sometimes I don't believe this truth. I feel as though my home could be bigger. My refrigerator could be more stocked. My energy level could be higher. Help me to remember that you are the giver of all good gifts. You are also the supplier of everything I need to do good in this hurting world. Day by day, remind me of who you are to me: Father, Savior, Lord, King, Ruler, Almighty God. In turn, help me to give with all I have to those who enter my home and to do so with a winsome, grateful, "happy spirit." Amen.

Grand Ideas

1. Look around your home and literally make room for your grandchildren by clearing out clutter or unused furniture, or redoing a spare room so they always have a place to stay.
2. As soon as you know your family is coming for a visit, start adjusting your food budget so you can buy some fun extras when they arrive.
3. As you look ahead to a visit, check your calendar and do your best to slow down in the days prior to their arrival so you will be well rested and ready for them.

Chapter 6

Nurturing the Grandparent-Grandchild *Relationship*

Do not let any unwholesome talk come out
of your mouths, but only what is helpful for
building others up according to their needs,
that it may benefit those who listen.

Ephesians 4:29

Before I speak, I must think about what you are
struggling with and what you most need. Do you need
encouragement, comfort, hope, direction, wisdom,
courage, rebuke, warning, forgiveness, patience,
teaching, correction, thanks, insight, or something
else? My words must be shaped by your need.

Tim Lane and Paul Tripp

I was driving my two older grandsons back to their
house, a quick fifteen-minute ride, after three full days
of fun while their parents were traveling with their
baby brother across the state for a job search. We had a
great time doing all the glorious summer activities we enjoy

every year living near the lake including swimming, biking, long walks in the woods, and ice cream each evening. Every night the boys would go to bed and I would crash onto my own as soon as I knew they were asleep. Needless to say, I was pretty tired by the end of the three days and the car trip home soon proved it.

There I was, reflecting on how well both boys got along— no major upsets, just wonderful grandma and grandkid memories in the making—when bam! One of the boys poked the other, and I heard the most piercing scream bellowing from the backseat. "He hit me in the eye!" My already overly weary nerves pitched a sudden fit of their own as I almost ran us off the road. I expected to turn around and see my grandson without his eye intact. Honest.

I quickly pulled off to the side of the road to check on them. I unbuckled my seat belt, leaned over into the backseat, and saw all eyes intact and blinking at me. Relief. Then, just as I was pulling back onto the road, the culprit poked his brother again. Another brain-splitting scream emanated from behind me, which startled me even more than before. I sternly told them to stop or we would end up in a real time hot mess in a deep ditch.

Silence ensued during the remainder of the trip to their house. This fact alone should have alerted me that something was amiss, but it didn't. I got out of the car, walked around to assist my younger grandson with his car seat, and he looked at me with eyes as big as saucers. I asked him if he was okay. He nodded unconvincingly. Then I realized I had never been stern with them before—ever. I took my grandson's hands in mine and assured him how much I loved him, but that I needed him to understand that causing a ruckus in the car (at least when this particular grandma is driving) could cause an accident. He nodded, more convincingly this time. I got him out his car seat and he gave me a big, smooshy hug that I returned with gusto.

I learned an important lesson that afternoon in the car. If I am to enjoy a loving, close, nurturing relationship with my grandchildren, every word I speak matters. It matters to them and it needs to matter to me. With every chance I'm offered, I need to ask myself: What are their needs at this moment? Do my grandchildren need encouragement, hope, assurance, courage, exhortation, a good word, or a simple hug? Maybe all of the above. It's my task to rightly hone in on their most pressing needs moment by moment, and then, by God's grace, meet those needs in the appropriate way.

Certainly, as in the scenario I described above, there are instances when I'm responsible for my grandchildren's safety, and I might have to use my grandmotherly voice of authority for their protection. However, I never need to yell, demean, or demand. Rather, I can use gentle but firm words to steer them toward making good choices. Developing a nurturing bond with grandchildren means I must be sensitive to each child's particular personality and discern what makes them tick. I need to be on the lookout for positive ways to motivate them to follow Jesus. To get the job done right requires time, effort, patience, and loads of God's grace and divine wisdom. The payoff? The dividends are life eternal and pleasure evermore!

🎀 *Take-away Action Thought*

I will use every word I speak to encourage my grandchildren. Negative, critical, careless words are never to be spoken to them, around them, or about them.

My Heart's Cry to You, O Lord

Help me, Father, to weigh my words rightly. Give me the wisdom I need to sensitively discern what each of my grandchildren needs most from me. I want to encourage their hearts with every word I say to them. I know that there will be moments when I won't always know how to lift their spirits, but you know. Holy Spirit, nudge and guide my speech so that I leave my grandchildren with more peace, hope, faith, and love than before. My desire is to steer their little hearts directly to you, Jesus. Be my Shepherd so I might have the joy and privilege of helping you shepherd them into your arms. Amen.

Grand Ideas

1. Before you even say hello, make it a habit to say a prayer for God's wisdom and discernment so that you know what your grandchildren need to hear from you most.

2. Make it your goal to build a strong, close bond with your grandchildren and use your words to nurture that relationship.

3. If you're not sure how to handle a sticky situation with your grandchildren, ask them directly what they need from you in that moment.

Chapter 7

Cheering on Grandchildren, Up Close and Personal (or Long-Distance)

Lift up your hands to him for the lives of your children.
Lamentations 2:19

*Experiences labeled as the worst things that
ever happened, over time become some of the
best. That's because God uses the painful, difficult
experiences of life for our ultimate good.*

Randy Alcorn

Suffering makes us sweet. It's true. None of us enjoys pain. But no one can deny that sorrows tend to do an amazing work within the deepest parts of us if, and only if, we turn to God in the midst of our struggles. Almost a year ago, when my oldest daughter announced they might be moving out of town, it took me a few days for the news to sink in. But then I began to grieve—through the spring, the summer, and even into the fall. I wasn't crying every day or into the night, but many mornings I woke up feeling sad for some reason. But then as I got up and started my day I'd realize why: Oh, yes, they are moving. It's real. It's happening.

Today marks six months since my daughter, her husband, and their sons (my grandsons) changed their home address. We weathered the initial move pretty well. Then, there were frequent trips back here for birthdays, holidays, and some personal business. But now, we're looking at a long stretch when I won't be seeing my grandsons other than via video chat. It feels brutal not knowing when I'll get to hug them, play with them, and just love on them in person. My heart still gets sad on some days. Other days, I do fine with this new life change. But on all days, no matter what I'm feeling, I ask the Lord to give me fresh ideas to cheer on my grandchildren from afar.

I don't want to get lost in the mire of missing them so much that it paralyzes me from becoming the kind of *grand*parent God intends. It is tempting on some particularly gloomy days for me to get busy doing anything and everything except think about how much I miss my little guys. But I know better. More importantly, I know God. He wants me to take this situation and transform it from one of the worst to something worth celebrating. But it won't happen until I lift up my hands to him in worship, thanks, praise, and surrender. Is it easy? No. Is it necessary? Absolutely.

God is and always has been in the life-transformation business. He takes our worst failings, most painful circumstances, and gut-wrenching regrets and transforms them for his glory and our good. More than anything, I want my grandchildren to learn this important biblical principle as early on as possible. I want them to learn to discipline their thoughts so that in those moments of great emotional upset they will never forget how much God loves them. My heart's desire is that I can, by my own example, instruct these little ones to turn directly to Jesus when they are hurting.

This means nudging them toward the love of God when they are sick, rejected, disappointed, hurt, confused, discouraged, in need, lonely, or without direction. Whatever their need, Jesus is their supply (as well as mine). Making this principle practical means that even when I'm not in physical proximity to my beloved grandchildren, I can't neglect to cheer them on. So, I write short notes for them each week (and I include a dollar bill in each one). I talk with them on the phone. Whenever an opportunity arises to video chat, I take it. The means of cheering on my grandchildren can't be counted. *Grand*parents must be at-the-ready, either to initiate contact or to invite it in. Cheering our grandchildren on is perhaps one of the most joyous ways we can demonstrate our love to them.

Take-away Action Thought

I will not allow time, lack of energy, or distance to hinder me from weekly contact in one form or another with my grandchildren. I will place reminders on my calendar so I won't forget to cheer on or cheer up my grandchildren.

My Heart's Cry to You, O Lord

I need your continual reminders that what I often view as the worst thing to happen can transform into something quite beautiful over time. Help me to keep eternity in mind whenever I start to feel downhearted or struggle to trust you with life's ever-changing circumstances. Father, I know that you are the master of transformation. Give me winsome ways to point my grandchildren to you when they are hurting. I want them to learn how to turn directly to you whenever they are in pain. Show me how to best cheer them on, Lord. If they are close by, give me practical ways to enter into their lives to demonstrate that I care. If they are far away, make me a creative *grand*parent who doesn't allow distance to stop me from finding fresh ways of encouraging them. Lord, thank you for the privilege of influencing this next generation. Amen.

Grand Ideas

1. If your grandchildren live nearby, ask their parents if you can spend a few hours each week with them.
2. If your grandchildren live far away, write a letter or text, phone, or video chat with them weekly.
3. Near or far, stay in as close of contact as you can so you know what they are facing each week (the good and the difficult), and tailor your communication with them to meet their specific needs.

Chapter 8

*Loving the Unique Individuality
of Each Grandchild*

Praise be to the God and Father of our Lord Jesus Christ,
the Father of compassion and the God of all comfort.

2 Corinthians 1:3

*You have a God who hears you, the power of love behind
you, the Holy Spirit within you, and all of heaven ahead
of you. If you have the Shepherd, you have grace for every
sin, direction for every turn, a candle for every corner, and
an anchor for every storm. You have everything you need.*

Max Lucado

We are in that "wait and see" stage with our new-est grandchild—our first granddaughter, Cha-ris, whose name means "grace." I marvel at the implications of her name and how richly grace will inform little Charis's life choices. Of course, a given name can be solely that: a name. Without love, vision, wisdom, or intention, a child can grow up never realizing the beauti-ful idea her name might suggest. It's up to the parents, grandparents, and every other interested party to make sure that children become productive adults for the sake of more than just helping society. Rather, as Christ followers, we want to instill in our children and grandchildren a greater vision and desire to live out the plan and purpose for which God brings them into this world, which is to know God and make him known.

As I watch my three grandsons grow and mature, one thing strikes me often and hard: each of them is so different. Despite being raised in the same house with the same parents and receiving the same love every day, each of these little men act and react uniquely to the world around them. While this might puzzle some, I am in awe. I view their individuality as living proof of the principles found in Psalm 139, which is that God formed each of them (and all of us) in a way that is pleasing to him and that gives him glory. How amazing.

In my interactions with these four little persons, I often quietly thank the Lord for this up close and personal opportunity to watch how he will shape and mold them. I have the honor of observing how God will use their varied gifts, talents, and yes, even limitations, for his glory and their good. It's a spectacular season of life—for them and for me. Because as long as I am here on this earth, I am blessed with the ability to see God do what he does best: train up and transform lives.

*Grand*parents never play favorites. Sure, I have to admit that my oldest grandson reaches places in my heart I didn't know existed. He is so much like me (and like his mom, who is also like me). There's a whole lot of loving going on here. But then my second grandson—one hundred percent my opposite—I find comical and charming. He is a real smoothie, and he knows how to endear himself to anyone he meets. Then there is grandson number three who is a lovely mix of his older two brothers, which I love. Finally, there is our one and only granddaughter who steals my heart with every smile. Enough said. I look at these four and think, "Kids come in all varieties, just like ice cream." And I do love many flavors of ice cream.

*Grand*parents must find unique or clever ways to emphasize and capitalize on their grandchild's strengths while using biblical principles to weaken the grasp of inherent and potential sin, which is not an easy task. Since *grand*parents are not parents, we must always be mindful of the fact that we are not in charge of disciplining our grandkids (with the exception of special circumstances). Thank the good Lord for that. Still, we have an awesome charge before us to gently, wisely, and courageously steer these young and pliable lives toward Jesus. We can't do this successfully unless we know our grandchildren intimately. Thus we should study their ways, watch for clues, talk with them, spend time with them, and invest in what they enjoy. After finding out what makes them tick, we take what we've observed straight to God to ask him for wisdom. As we do, we are reminded that God has given us everything we need to face when we look first to him, our Creator and loving heavenly Father.

𝒫ℛ Take-away Action Thought

I will study my grandchildren's personalities, their likes/dislikes, and their actions/reactions so I can effectively steer them toward the ways of Jesus. I will also remind them that they have everything they need in Jesus.

My Heart's Cry to You, O Lord

Help me, Father, to rightly discern what my grandchildren need most from me. Give me your heavenly wisdom to understand their strengths and weaknesses, so I can gently guide them back to you with biblical truth. I realize that every person has a unique personality and that each of us responds differently to life's circumstances. Our personalities have specific strengths and weaknesses, but you use both to mature and mold us into the image of Jesus. Please help me to use my words rightly and righteously. Never allow me to speak anything to my grandchildren that would make them believe I am favoring one over another. I want them to know that I love each of them with one hundred percent of my heart. Amen.

Grand Ideas

1. Make a study of each of your grandchildren, using your guidance and wisdom to know how to effectively open their tender hearts to you.

2. Though grandchildren are all different, learn how to praise each one according to their specific strengths and weaknesses.

3. If you ever begin to show preference for one grandchild over another, step up your love (in word and deed) for the other(s).

Chapter 9

Accepting Unconditionally with Open Arms

This is love: not that we loved God, but that he loved us
and sent his Son as an atoning sacrifice for our sins.

1 John 4:10

*Does God love us because of our goodness? Because
of our kindness? Because of our great faith? No,
he loves because of his goodness, kindness, and
great faith. John says, it like this: "This is love:
not that we loved God, but that he loved us."*

Max Lucado

Unfortunately, it's not unusual to see grandparents
who love their grandchildren only when they feel
loved by them. I've witnessed this sad scenario
time and again. A grandparent runs headlong toward their
young grandchild, arms extended and letting out a shrill
sound as they fruitlessly attempt to snatch their progeny
from the parent's arms. Of course, the child begins wailing,
while trying to crawl inside the safety net of the parent's
embrace. What happens next? The grandparent starts com-
plaining that the child doesn't love them. What?

How would any of us adults feel in the same situation as the poor child? We'd be looking for the nearest escape route too. No one likes to be pounced on. What I'd like to say to these unwitting grandparents is this: Treat your grandchildren with the same dignity and respect you expect of others. Just because they are small in stature doesn't mean they don't feel exactly as you would if attacked with too much enthusiasm. We would all be screaming, silently or aloud, "Personal space! Please respect my personal space!"

Taken even further, I've heard far too many grandparents play the "Woe is me!" game to anyone within earshot. "My grandchildren don't love me. They won't even give me a hug when I see them. What's wrong with me? What did I do to make them hate me?" Though it's sad to admit, the truth is that when folks speak this way they are announcing to the world that they are inappropriately (and sinfully) dependent upon the ever-changing whims and expressions of love from children. *Grand*parents, by comparison, are mirror opposites. *Grand*parents courteously wait for their grandchildren to get acclimated to their presence. They don't pounce; they display patience. They don't take as personal their grandchildren's lack of physical or emotional reaction, because the child's emotional state is as changeable as the weather. They understand that children don't always behave like mature adults. In short, *grand*parents offer unconditional acceptance, open arms, and grace upon grace.

Grace upon grace. Unconditional love. Total acceptance. Open arms. These are only a few of the attitudes and actions that make *grand*parents so different from folks who assume a casual role as a grandparent. Which would you rather be: A seemingly insignificant bystander who shows up now and then with a gift but with two closed fists that demand affection from the grandchildren before letting go of the goods; or someone who views every opportunity to interact with their grandchildren as having potential eternal impact and takes their love as it comes, without offense? I know I'd rather be the latter.

*Grand*parenting entails loving your grandchildren, even if it takes long years for them to ever demonstrate that same kind of love toward you. *Grand*parents don't give up on their grandchildren when they go through rough patches and routinely disappoint those around them. No, *grand*parents keep praying, forgiving, loving, hoping, and being kind, generous, gentle, and persistent in their commitment toward their grandchildren. *Grand*parents never give up on their grandchildren. They do not stop interceding for their grandchildren through word or deed until their prayers are answered. That, my friends, is the *grand*est gesture of all.

Take-away Action Thought

When my grandchildren are going through difficult times and don't seem to love me (or others) as I would hope, I will pray for them and look for fresh (and frequent) ways to demonstrate their immense value to me.

My Heart's Cry to You, O Lord

Father, when my wonderful grandchildren interact with each other, their parents, and me, I see evidence that we are all sinful human beings in need of your forgiveness and grace. Help me to be consistent in offering forgiveness, lots of grace, unconditional love, and acceptance toward them as they grow. My utmost desire is that my grandchildren will come to a saving faith in Jesus at an early age. Please, Lord, grant my request. I know that it is only with your Holy Spirit within us and protecting us (potentially even from ourselves) that we can have abundant life here on earth. I pray that you will create tender, teachable hearts in my grandchildren and that the world and its riches will not squelch their longing for you above all else. Amen.

Grand Ideas

1. When your grandchildren behave unkindly, consistently show unconditional love toward them.
2. At those points when your grandchildren struggle to make sense of life, diligently intercede in prayer for them.
3. Be on the lookout for practical ways to demonstrate your support of your grandchildren.

Chapter 10

Being a Never-Fail Safety Net

No discipline seems pleasant at the time, but painful.
Later on, however, it produces a harvest of righteousness
and peace for those who have been trained by it.

Hebrews 12:11

*Suffering makes hearts tender and gives us greater love
for others. The résumé of every encourager and every
counselor contains suffering. Only the wounded can serve.*

Randy Alcorn

I love the above quote from Randy Alcorn. Why? Because it's true, and it helps to rightly frame our pain and suffering in the lens of eternity. Rather than look back and wince as we recall our own early childhood moments of pain, helplessness, regret, confusion, hopelessness— you name it—today's *grand*parents view those memories as instructional. We look back, and we remember how we felt when someone hurt our feelings, rejected our friendship, told untruths about us, misunderstood us, demeaned us, sabotaged us, or even spewed hatred toward us. If we reframe the scenario in light of what we learned about God, about ourselves, and about how to handle pain in a biblical way, those experiences will provide us with wisdom.

Though we would rather have not gone through these seasons of growing pains, we must recognize that nothing comes to us that hasn't first been sifted through the hands of God. We must embrace the truth that God can and will transform evil into good, for his glory and, ultimately, our good. As I look back to my own childhood, I can recall in vivid detail times when both strangers and friends said crushingly awful words to me. As time passed, however, the lens of eternity has become clearer to me. I'm able to recognize that every ill-spoken word and roll of the eyes sent in my direction made me more compassionate, kinder, gentler, and more patient. To God be the glory! With the intervening strength and grace of the Holy Spirit, *grand*-parents can overcome their own painful pasts and minister lovingly to their grandchildren, using those lessons. It's all a matter of perspective.

Today's *grand*parents have the unique and privileged role of being the resident never-fail safety net for their grandchildren. Whether your grandchildren need an adult to drive them to an after-school event, listen to them recount their day, or vent about how they don't believe their parents understand them anymore—if we're there for them during these moments, then we'll have a golden opportunity to display compassion, to listen, and to share how God can take the worst we endure and use it for good. I believe we underestimate the power of healing that can take place when we simply listen. Most of the time, we cannot alter our grandchildren's circumstances. We can, however, hone our listening skills so that our grandchildren are confident they have our full attention and support.

So what does effective listening look and sound like? To effectively hear what someone is saying is a difficult skill to master. It takes loads of effort and self-discipline to not jump in mid-sentence when another person is talking. It requires concentration—which means no peeks at the television or smart phones. To listen effectively, *grand*parents must set aside all distractions, pray for help and wisdom, place themselves in their grandchild's shoes (this is when a swift recalling of your own childhood pains is helpful), and choose their words with care (remembering that less words are always better than too many). By learning to listen well, *grand*parents demonstrate that there isn't another person in the world they would rather be listening to, there isn't another place they would rather be, and nothing is more important than hearing their grandchildren share what's happening in their lives. In that moment, the only person who matters is that grandchild.

Take-away Action Thought

When my grandchildren come to me with their problems, complaints, and struggles, I will set aside whatever I am doing and give them my full attention for as long as they need my listening ear.

My Heart's Cry to You, O Lord

Dear Jesus, help me to become a better listener every day. Give me the gentle nudges I need so I can truly hear what my grandchildren are saying and what they need from me. I am tempted to jump ahead and interrupt others when they're speaking to me. Instead of just listening, I prepare how I want to answer them. Lord, I know that when I do this I'm not fully engaged with what my grandchildren are trying to tell me. Give me complete concentration and a compassionate and gentle heart. Help me use my past pain and suffering to build a bridge of love with my grandchildren. Use my past mistakes and hurts to reach into their hearts. Lord, I know that you are the master of transforming evil into good. Please do this for me and for my grandchildren. Amen.

Grand Ideas

1. When your grandchildren come to you in distress, invite them to sit down and talk through their problems.
2. As you listen to them speak, don't interrupt them. Instead, patiently give them all the time and attention they need so they feel loved and understood.
3. Even when you disagree with what your grandchildren may say, keep your opinions to yourself until you're asked to do otherwise!

Part Two
Why Are Grandparents Essential?

 *Chapter 11*

Grandparents Can Take the Time

My times are in your hands.

Psalm 31:15

When you try to solve human problems with human resources in your human strength, there will never be enough. However, if you would like to follow Me and work with Me, I will meet the deepest needs around you and in you and through you with unending resources in supernatural, all-powerful strength.

Jennie Allen

Not too long ago, I woke up in the middle of the night and wondered how I would be able to complete everything I needed to do. Since I work from home, people tend to think that I have all the time in the world—but this isn't true. While my schedule is flexible, my free time is sparse. Like everyone else, I have to juggle my work, family, church, and other responsibilities (which often take more time than all of the above combined). I'm just blessed not have a boss looming over my shoulder, making sure I finish my projects before the deadlines. All that to say we never really know how busy someone is from the outside looking in.

But what we can know comes straight from Scripture—Psalm 31:15 to be exact: Our times are in the hands of the Lord. This verse begs the question of how *grand*parents are to spend their hours and days. As a middle-aged or older adult with grandchildren, how do you prioritize your time? Family first, work second, leisure third, church fourth, other fifth? Be honest. Take a long look at last month and review what you did every day. If you're like me, you squandered some time doing nothing in particular. While this isn't wrong, I could have chosen to "squander" those few hours with my grandchildren.

Of course, some people may need some space for themselves, which is perfectly healthy. But we all need to ask ourselves if some of our "extra" leisure time could be better spent being with our grandchildren.

Time: We all have the same amount of it, yet some seem to get so much more out of their portion than others. I like to keep Ephesians 5:15–16 in the forefront of my mind—it admonishes Christ followers to stay alert and make the most of the time at hand, because the days are evil. Most of us would gladly give up a few particular time-consuming activities in favor of spending more time with our grandchildren. But at what cost? And what about activities we enjoy? Are we willing to say no to that third round of golf in one week or to working in the garden? What about inviting our grandchildren to join us in our favorite activities and teach them what we love to do and why?

One of the most effective impetuses to help us be more engaged with our grandchildren is to recall our own early parenting years. How fast those years flew by. How bone weary we felt in the midst of them. How often we tried to squeeze in extra moments for making memories, but duty called: dinner, cleaning, laundry, and so on. How we longed for someone to kindly swoop in and give us a break. Busy from morning until night. The end of the many parenting responsibilities was never in sight.

*Grand*parents remember all this and then do something about it—that is, we help lighten our children's load by spending time with their children. Although we all need some "fun time" for ourselves, maybe we can figure out a way to include the grandchildren because, let's be honest, kids in general know instinctively how to have fun in ways that some of us adults may have forgotten.

Time. We all have the same amount of it. Precisely the same. So let's take a good hard look at how we choose to spend our hours and ask the Lord to direct us toward what (or who) matters most. We already know how busy everyone is, but *grand*parents understand that time is a commodity we can invest wisely, with eternity in mind.

Take-away Action Thought

I will make a list of all my activities to help me better understand how I choose to spend the time I have. If I'm not investing enough time with my family, I will drop out of unnecessary engagements and commitments.

My Heart's Cry to You, O Lord

Help me to be a prudent time manager. I want to invest my hours, my energy, and my resources into that which will last forever. Only by putting you first and listening to the Holy Spirit's direction can I use my time in a way that pleases you. Help me to recall how weary and overwhelmed I felt when I was in the thick of my parenting years. Show me how and when it's appropriate for me to care for my grandchildren so that my adult children can take a break. Make me sensitive to how I can use my time to draw my grandchildren closer to you—and that can't happen if I don't spend time with them. Amen.

Grand Ideas

1. Periodically and honestly assess how you spend your days. Then make the necessary changes if your priorities are skewed.
2. When you make plans, consistently create space on your calendar for your grandchildren.
3. Even if your grandchildren have such busy schedules that they don't have time to spend with you, get creative by offering to drive them to and from their events.

Chapter 12

Grandparents Can See What Parents Sometimes Miss

You are the light of the world. A town built on a hill cannot be hidden. Neither do people light a lamp and put it under a bowl. Instead they put it on its stand, and it gives light to everyone in the house. In the same way, let your light shine before others, that they may see your good deeds and glorify your Father in heaven.

Matthew 5:14–16

We live in a culture that will exercise its influence on every area of our lives. As we seek to prepare them (our grandchildren), we need to be humbly honest about the places where our own lifestyles have been more shaped by cultural norms than by biblical principles. We cannot disciple our (grandchildren) into a consistently biblical lifestyle without being willing to evaluate the places where our own lives are inconsistent.

Paul Tripp

*M*any long years ago when my now twenty-six-year-old son was a toddler, I instructed him to do something and was promptly ignored. My father, who was watching all this, looked at me and said, "He sure doesn't listen very well." I wearily nodded in response. I had given birth to four children within a span of six years, and I often felt as though I was either carrying a baby inside of me or nursing one. Those early parenting years were and still are a blur to me. Of course, I was worn so thin and tired that I remember thinking to my overly exhausted self, "I really should get up and chase my son and make him obey, but I'm so tired. . ."

Over the next few months, I learned that if I put in the extra effort to make him mind me, it would be easier in the long run. Parenting uses every ounce of mental, emotional, and physical reserve we have stored up inside of us until nothing is left.

With that knowledge, as a *grand*parent, I tend to be sensitive to when my grandchildren don't obey their parents. As my adult children parent their children, I applaud their effort, sacrifices, and commitment. However, I can spot some warning signs they may miss because I've been there, done that, and observed similar attitudes in my own children. *Grand*parents of vision wisely take note of the good, the bad, and the ugly. While they aren't out to catch their grandchildren in the act of doing something naughty, they are sensitive to potentially problematic attitudes and actions.

It is a delicate position to be in when a *grand*parent sees a beloved grandchild exhibiting sinful behavior and the parents don't recognize it. Do we intervene or not? Do we approach our grandchild directly or not? Do we walk away and pray? Much depends on the kind of relationship we have with our adult children. Have they given us permission to gently correct their children? Have they assured us that they want to know if we observe bad behavior or sinful speech?

Answering these questions will give *grand*parents the guidance they need as to what to do and say when they witness their grandchildren misbehaving or going down a dangerous path. *Grand*parents won't merely be on the lookout for naughty behavior. For the most part, they will be eager to spot and encourage good attitudes, helpful hands, a servant's spirit, and a happy countenance. The bulk of observations should focus on all the small, seemingly insignificant positive choices our grandchildren make. With our encouragement, their good behavior will develop into lifetime habits and principles by which they will govern themselves. So the next time you're with your grandchildren, have your eyes peeled for the smallest good word, deed, or attitude of the heart. When you notice someone doing right, praise them for it. Then they will be all the more likely to repeat it.

Take-away Action Thought

When I am with my grandchildren, I will be alert for the good things they do. When I see them making the right choice, I will praise and encourage them.

My Heart's Cry to You, O Lord

Father, open my eyes to see when my grandchildren do good. Instead of honing in on their mistakes and failings, help me to be the *grand*parent who cheers them on when they make godly choices, no matter how small. Be with me, Lord, and guide my heart and thoughts so I pay attention when I'm with them. If there are occasions when I observe my grandchildren disobeying, help me to handle the situation with gentleness and grace. Give me the wisdom to stop myself if I ever overstep my boundaries. Teach me to be a good observer and then to bring it all to you in prayer. Amen.

Grand Ideas

1. If and when you see one of your grandchildren disobeying or speaking in ungodly ways, be sure to pray before you respond.
2. Sensitively initiate a conversation with your adult children about how they would like you to handle sinful behavior you observe when you're caring for your grandchildren.
3. When you spend time with your grandchildren, be on the lookout for ways you can offer them praise for good decisions, both large and small.

Chapter 13

Grandparents Can Lighten the Family Load

For Christ's love compels us.

2 Corinthians 5:14

Insightful people are insightful not because
they have the right answers but because
they have asked the right questions.

Paul Tripp

I have loads of ideas running through my brain on any given day, which is why I often check myself before jumping headlong into my latest bright idea. It's not that I would describe myself as impulsive; I'm the opposite. When it comes to some fun idea to help out my children and grandchildren, however, I'm all for it.

While most of my creative plans are greeted with excitement, I do recall a few instances when I thought I was doing someone a favor because I assumed I knew what they needed—or, more accurately, wanted—without asking them. Although my heart was in the right place, I failed to take into account some details that would have altered how I chose to lend a hand—if I had only been aware. Nowadays, I still happily ponder gifts to buy, memories to make, and investments to start with friends and family alike. However, I've learned my lesson from some epic failures in the past. Today, when I see a need that has to be met and the love of Christ compels me to help, I ask before I act.

I've learned to take the extra time to inquire more fully into a situation before setting into motion my grand plans. I will first contact the person I want to assist and then offer them my suggestion. After my proposal, I now ask for their permission to proceed, and I let them know I'm open to their ideas of how to help them. This new, improved process makes all the difference. For one, I know I'm meeting their most urgent need. Second, I'm not left wondering if I missed the mark or hit it square on. There are bonuses for both parties when there is clear communication about what is actually needed and appreciated.

*Grand*parents are *grand* because they are ready and willing to lighten the load of their adult children. They don't wait around for their children to contact them. If they notice that something needs doing that they can do, they offer up their help. Simple. *Grand*parents never scoff at doing menial labor. If they are able, they will happily do the laundry, unload the dishwasher, take out the trash, feed the dogs, or run to the drug store if a grandchild needs medicine.

*Grand*parents are *grand* because they are not complainers (aloud or in their hearts). They understand how utterly exhausting parenting can be, and they gladly do what needs doing if they can be of assistance. *Grand*parents learn to cultivate a flexible relationship that is as easy-going as possible for everyone. They don't make others walk on egg-shells around them. Instead, they cheerfully and frequently offer their assistance with no strings attached.

*Grand*parents are *grand* because they are eager to spend time with their grandchildren and are willing to lighten the family load so that the parents can have more quality time with their children. *Grand*parents are open-minded, big-hearted, and generally wonderful people to have around. But remember: as in every area of life, begin with baby-steps and grow into the kind of *grand*parent you hope to be. None of us can be all things to all people, but we do what we can with the resources and gifts that God places with us.

Take-away Action Thought

When I see a way to lighten my family's load, I will offer my help with no strings attached. I will be flexible to do whatever needs doing—with a joyful heart.

My Heart's Cry to You, O Lord

Help me, Father, to be sensitive to my adult children and my grandchildren and offer assistance when they are in need. Make me a happily flexible *grand*parent, who is willing to do whatever is most required. Remind me to ask the right questions so that I understand how to best serve my adult children. Even when they say no to me, don't let me take it personally. I want to be available as much as I can to help, but I also need to respect healthy boundaries and the fact that my adult children have their own ways. I pray that we will continuously nurture open, kind, and mutually respectful relationships between us. Amen.

Grand Ideas

1. Even if you think you know what your adult children need most, respectfully ask them first.
2. When your adult children face a hectic and exhausting season of parenting, offer your time and talents to ease their load.
3. Before your adult children become overwhelmed by the stresses of life and parenting, open the doors of communication between you, and then remind them that you are always ready to be of assistance.

Chapter 14

Grandparents Can Offer Perspective

The words of the reckless pierce like swords,
but the tongue of the wise brings healing.

Proverbs 12:18

*People respond positively to those who refuse to
be unempathetic, impatient, resentful, envious,
intolerant, unmindful, and anti-social or the
bully, retaliator, self-appointed prosecutor, rebel
and abuser. Even so, there are three good reasons
why we should communicate kindly. It's about who
I am, who the other person is, and who God is.*

Emerson Eggerichs

I sat listening to a group of young moms swapping stories about their kids: funny stories, sad stories, irritat-
ing stories, and desperately crazy stories. That is the
beauty of female fellowship—most of us have been there,
done that, and can heartily join in the conversational fray.
To the delight of fellow mothers (and grandmothers), the
majority of tales told are heavy on the positive side. But

when one mother shares her story and it tilts toward the negative, everyone's ears perk up. After all, we want to help each other.

During one such occasion, a mother in her thirties started talking about her middle son and his latest she-nanigans. Mind you, what she told us wasn't within the norms of "that's just a boy" behavior. Her son was acting cruelly, violently, even hatefully toward her and their other children. She seemed scared of being with her son, and she told us she was afraid of being home alone with him. She wasn't afraid of *him*, but she was afraid of losing her temper to the point of lashing out in frustration.

We all listened carefully, interjected at appropriate mo-ments, offered what advice we could to this hurting woman, and then prayed for her. Afterward, we encouraged biblical counseling through trusted local Christian sources and as-sured her she could call on us day or night as needed. But perhaps the most helpful task we undertook was to help her see the good in her son. By asking pointed questions and listening well to her replies, we discovered some very positive aspects to this young man she had been missing. It was almost as though a veil lifted and she had fresh eyes of love for her son. What changed? Perspective. Sometimes we get lost in our circumstances and become so distressed and emotional that we need others who will speak truth and eternal perspective into our situation.

Cue in the *grand*parents who come to the rescue of frazzled, anxious, worn-out parents in need of a fresh perspective. *Grand*parents can indeed come to the rescue of the family when they take the time to recognize troublesome situations and analyze them from a new angle. *Grand*parents—by virtue of their age, experience, and wisdom—know that a person's story isn't over until the final page is written. They understand that wayward children can outgrow their sinful ways and change dramatically.

Whenever a new family unit is established, there usually is one child in the mix who will be a challenge. You know them, and maybe you were even one of them back in the day! They are easy to spot: Overly opinionated, not too keen on taking directions, and opposed to doing things any way but their own. These rambunctious children can get into a lot of hot water. Instead of praise, they hear only rebuke: "No, don't do that! What is going on here? What were you thinking?"

Enter in *grand*parents who see the same issues in their grandchildren as they did in their own children. Unlike their children, though, they have the needed long-range perspective to see far beyond today's temporary distresses. They also have the energy and distance required to love their grandchildren with gusto, regardless of whether they act out in negative ways. *Grand*parents of faith go straight to God for his wisdom to win their grandchildren over. They intercede every day on behalf of their welfare. When they are with their grandchildren, *grand*parents always find something positive and kind to say to them. They know the lasting power a good word has on little ones (and big ones!).

🌿 *Take-away Action Thought*

When I see my grandchildren acting out in negative ways, I will first pray for them. Then I will praise them for something, even if requires effort and creativity on my part.

My Heart's Cry to You, O Lord

Help me, Lord, to find uplifting words to speak to my grandchildren. Even though there will be times when one (or more) will act out or sin, help me praise them for their good qualities. I believe we are all greatly affected by the words spoken to us and about us. Help me also to keep this principle at the forefront of my mind, so I can have the long-term eternal perspective that encourages my adult children when they struggle to see the good in their child. Help me remember the times when I felt the same discouragement while parenting, and remind me of the ways you eventually brought about a wonderful change. Above all, let every word I speak bring honor to you. Amen.

Grand Ideas

1. You are most likely at an age when you have seen even the worst behavior transformed over time by the power of God. Never stop praying or lose hope for any of your grandchildren, no matter what they say or how they act.

2. Be especially tenderhearted toward your adult children, who may grow weary raising a challenging child. Speak only words of encouragement to them about their children.
3. As you watch my grandchildren interact with others, intentionally speak positive words that will encourage them to do better when they falter.

# Chapter 15

Grandparents Can Step in During Seasons of Sickness

Those who go out weeping,
carrying seed to sow,
will return with songs of joy,
carrying sheaves with them.

Psalm 126:6

God asks us to do things by faith. He wants us to trust Him, no matter what circumstances we find ourselves in. Nothing more, nothing less. The journey we are on is designed to help us trust God in ways we don't expect and can't foresee.

Heidi St. John

I hate being sick, and I do all I can in order to stay healthy. Yet, I will be the first to admit that I feel my dependence on the Lord more keenly during times of illness or pain. It's in the midst of sleepless nights when I toss and turn and hurt too much to go back to sleep that I draw nearer to God in prayer. Although I know this can be good, I still find myself resisting pain or illness when it comes my way.

Several good friends of mine are now caring for their adult children or their grandchildren. In one of the circumstances, it is a physical illness that places my friend in a position of caregiver. In the other situations, my friends are caring for their grandchildren because of the spiritual sickness of their adult children. In all these cases, I believe (as do my wonderful friends) that God is doing good and necessary work in the lives of these adult children and their grandchildren.

I've listened to my friends share their heartbreaking stories of how alcohol and drugs have taken their children captive. Their children have lost careers, homes, cars, bank accounts, family—the list goes on. While these adult children are on the road to recovery, my friends have helped bridge the gap with continual prayer and by opening their homes once again to these adult children. Other friends now have custody of their grandchildren because their adult children cannot (or, in some cases, will not) parent responsibly. Pain and sickness arrive in many guises, leaving a trail of heartache. But as long as people like my friends live and breathe, there is hope, faith, and love—especially with God.

*Grand*parents are those selfless individuals willing to step up and in for the family's greater good during these seasons of illness. Whether the sickness is physical, mental, emotional, spiritual, or a combination, *grand*parents know that God will supply their every need, one day at a time. I've known quite a few widowed *grand*mothers who are caring for their grandchildren. These brave souls are well into their retirement years, and yet they have taken on the high calling of parenting their grandchildren. Now that these children live in a loving and safe place, they are making good progress in school and at home. I feel I can help by lifting them all up in prayer, especially that God will give them strength to cope in their new roles as replacement parents.

I also have friends who have opened their homes to their adult children and their grandchildren while the adult children recover from sickness. One friend is nursing her son back to health after a car accident. Another friend's daughter is living with her after having a difficult birth and a husband who is constantly traveling. A different friend is now caring for her four grandsons while her daughter undergoes cancer treatment. Names, places, and circumstances may vary, but there is one constant that runs through their lives: Their selfless sacrifice for their children and grandchildren. In sickness or in health, *grand*parents like these live up to their special title.

Take-away Action Thought

When a need arises for providing care for one of my children or grandchildren, I'll look for ways that I can make a difference.

My Heart's Cry to You, O Lord

Father, tune me in to the needs of my adult children and grandchildren. I want to be aware of special circumstances that may warrant me taking over some of the caregiving. Help me know when to sensitively offer help to my children. Whether their need is physical, mental, emotional, or spiritual, show me what to do. Lord, only you truly understand each individual's deepest hurts and hidden pain. Please guide me with your divine wisdom and make me aware of when and how I can help others, all the while showing your love, grace, and gentleness as I go. Amen.

Grand Ideas

1. If the need arises for you to invite your adult children or grandchildren into your home for a season, do so, but also take the time to determine (through a family meeting) the terms of their visit.

2. If your grandchildren are ever in need of a home, temporarily or permanently, prayerfully consider taking on the role of parenting again until your adult children are able.

3. Talk to other grandparents who have stepped in and cared for their adult children or grandchildren. Find out specifically what they did to make their living arrangements successful.

Chapter 16

Grandparents Can Take Charge When Adult Children Can't

For if you forgive other people when they sin against you,
your heavenly Father will also forgive you.
But if you do not forgive others their sins,
your Father will not forgive your sins.

Matthew 6:14–15

*To forgive the incessant provocations of daily life—to
keep on forgiving the bossy mother-in-law, the bullying
husband, the nagging wife, the selfish daughter, the
deceitful son—how can we do it? Only, I think, by
remembering where we stand, by meaning our words
when we say in our prayers each night, 'Forgive us
our trespasses as we forgive those that trespass against
us.' We are offered forgiveness on no other terms. To
refuse it is to refuse God's mercy for ourselves. There is
no hint of exceptions and God means what he says.*

C. S. Lewis

I believe that God brings courageous people across our paths so we can observe firsthand what true selflessness, Christ-honoring servanthood, and miracles in the making look like. In just the past few years, I've listened to men and women tell me how they have had to take custody of their grandchildren because their adult child couldn't stay clean, sober, employed, out of casinos, or focused long enough to create a remotely safe home for their children.

My friends have gone through the long and painful process of multiple court hearings, where they have had to retell and rehash the horrendous details of neglect, abuse, and child endangerment in front of a judge and a room full of strangers. Sadly, not all public servants are gracious to grandparents interfering in their negligent adult children's destructive lifestyles. Instead of receiving encouragement and sympathy for courageously fighting for the betterment of their grandchildren's lives, they are verbally abused, threatened, and subjected to unwarranted aggression by court officials.

Yet, they never give up. Time and time again these *grand*parents step up and into their roles as advocates for their grandchildren. Some of these *grand*parents have to take even more drastic measures to protect their grandchildren with restraining orders. Some must live vigilantly, constantly protecting their grandchildren from being kidnapped by their troubled adult children. Others have adopted their grandchildren and are revisiting all the earlier-in-life parental decisions they never dreamed they would have to make again. What school should their grandchildren attend? What doctor should they go to? How do they financially support a child? Will they be able to help them pay for college? Yet, these *grand*parents take on parenting some twenty years past their prime and do so with amazing stamina and grit. All because of their love for their grandchildren.

Of the countless conversations I've had with those friends of mine who have taken over raising their grandchildren, one struggle rises to the top: "It is so hard to forgive our adult child when we are paying the price for their poor choices." Since the whole painful scenario of raising one's grandchildren arose because of the adult child's lack of ability to do so, blame can fast-track itself into *grand*parents' hearts and minds. *Grand*parents can struggle to keep their hearts and minds free of resentment and bitterness when they are the ones paying the price—and a heavy one it is—for their child's irresponsibility.

This negativity can swiftly take on a life of its own after *grand*parents start to discover more and more emotional fallout as time presses on. Understandably, the grandchildren are emotionally broken, spiritually bereft, and physically sick. With this rising tide of problems comes a justifiable anger at the adult child's choices. Of all the possible responses *grand*parents could take against their children, this statement seems to be the healthiest and most profound: "Until I asked God for the grace and the desire to forgive, I felt as trapped and undone as my neglectful adult child." Forgiveness is a daily choice we all have to make. No matter how painful our life circumstances are,

God's word instructs us to forgive so that we will be forgiven. After all, we are only free of the pain inflicted upon us (or someone we love) after we've forgiven the perpetrator.

Take-away Action Thought

Whenever I begin to rehearse the wrong done to me or my grandchildren, I will immediately take these harmful thoughts to the Lord in prayer and ask him for the grace to fully forgive so that I can be free.

My Heart's Cry to You, O Lord

Help me to grasp the deepness of my sin that Jesus forgave on the cross. Never let me forget that I am no different from the worst of sinners. Yet I have been forgiven, and that is a precious, eternal gift. Place in me the desire and mercy to freely offer forgiveness to my children, even when daily insults, injuries, or painful responsibilities are thrown my way because of their irresponsibility. Constantly pull me back to you for care and keeping. I want to forgive, I need to forgive, and I must forgive, but I cannot do it without you. Amen.

Grand Ideas

1. Honestly assess the state of your heart and ask the Lord to reveal any pockets of unforgiveness within you.

2. When you begin to feel angry, resentful, or bitter against your adult child because of how his or her poor choices have negatively affected your life, go to God and beg for the supernatural grace to fully forgive that child.

3. As you seek to repair the damage done to your grandchildren because of your adult child's bad choices, seek to be an example to your grandchildren by forgiving their parents.

Chapter 17

Grandparents Can Show Tough Love

Though he brings grief, he will show compassion,
so great is his unfailing love. For he does not
willingly bring affliction or grief to anyone.

Lamentations 3:32–33

*While we tend to live for the pursuit of our happiness,
you are committed to the pursuit of our holiness. Teach
us that when we pursue only happiness we will lose
it along with holiness, but when we find holiness,
including the holiness that can come to us through
difficulties we will find the happiness of Heaven.*

Randy Alcorn

A couple I know are *grand*parents in every sense of the word. They have legally adopted their granddaughter, whom they've been caring for over the past three years. Though the child is only five years old and doesn't remember much about her father, she still cries for her daddy when a memory of him is triggered. These *grand*parents are faced with the difficult task of trying to simultaneously protect their granddaughter and help her understand why she cannot see her father. It's one of the most heartrending situations they have ever faced.

Their son, incarcerated for using and selling drugs, would drop his little girl off at my friends' house and not come back for days. Then, without explanation, he would end up at their doorstep and want to take away his little girl. A few days or possibly a week later, he would show up with their granddaughter in a filthy, disheveled, starving, and nonresponsive state. My friends appealed to their son time and again to get help for his drug addiction while they cared for their granddaughter, but he repeatedly refused.

This cycle continued until the legal system finally stepped in and charged him with numerous illegal activities. Only then did he give up custody of his daughter (whose mother was having issues of her own and therefore not involved) to my friends' care. Although my friends believed the worst was over, it wasn't. They now wrestle with repeatedly saying no to their son's emotional pleas to see his daughter while in jail. The one and only time they took her to see him ended badly and she cried for days afterward. As a result, my friends often feel as though they have to choose between meeting the needs of their granddaughter and those of their son. Situations like these prove that tough love is just as tough on those administering it as those receiving it.

*Grand*parents, like these two individuals described above, must look past the temporary inconvenience of today to the long tomorrow of eternity. Despite our pursuits to do this, we tend to automatically look for shortcuts to bring happiness to our children and grandchildren when God is asking something much harder but ultimately much better of us. Administering tough love is neither easy nor pain-free. But it is needed to protect, nurture, and strengthen those whom we love.

Through prayer, God will help us determine how to handle situations that require us to state an ultimatum, say no, determine healthy boundaries, or even deny entrance if the safety of a grandchild is being compromised. *Grand*parents must rely on God's sustaining strength to ensure the well-being of their grandchildren. No one looks forward to being placed in such a heart-wrenching position, yet sometimes God calls us into life-altering situations for the sake of the greater good.

Take-away Action Thought

When my grandchildren are at risk, I will lean on the Lord for the strength to protect them, even if that means denying my own adult children what they want.

My Heart's Cry to You, O Lord

Father, open my ears to hear what the Holy Spirit is guiding me to say and do during difficult situations with my adult children and grandchildren. I would never willingly enter into a situation where I must decide to protect my grandchildren over my adult child. But if the occasion arises, I must. If and when my adult child is able to resume parenting their children, give me the peace and strength to happily hand the responsibility back over to them. Give me your wisdom, strength, and grace to handle awkward, unnatural situations like those, if necessary. Gently guide me down the path you call me to, one day at a time. Amen.

Grand Ideas

1. When it is a matter of your grandchildren's safety, do what is necessary to keep them safe—even if that means keeping your adult child from them.
2. If you are placed in a situation where you must take legal custody of your grandchildren, seek out a community of other grandparents to give you the support you need.
3. If you feel threatened by your adult child, don't be afraid to use the weight of the law to protect yourself and your grandchildren.

Chapter 18

Grandparents Can Create a Safe Haven

Let anyone who is thirsty come to me and drink.

John 7:37

God is a God who opens the door and waves His hand, pointing pilgrims to a full table. His invitation is not just for a meal, however. It is for life. An invitation to come into His kingdom and take up residence in a tearless, graveless, painless world. Who can come? Whoever wishes. The invitation is at once universal and personal.

Max Lucado

I've thought for years now that the most impactful, relationship-building conversations happen around the dinner table. Food and family forge a strong union. *Grand*parents who are keenly aware of the spiritual consequences to every choice intentionally open wide their doors to their grandchildren. They point them to a full table. They offer them not simply any drink, but the drink that quenches every thirst: Jesus. Don't you love the picture this setting creates?

*Grand*parents not only open their home in hospitality, but they also open their hearts to transparent, genuine conversation. They are not afraid of communication that takes everyone at the table into deep waters. In fact, *grand*parents hope that will happen—and often. *Grand*parents seek to create a safe haven within their four walls. They cultivate loving, accepting, and trusting relationships. They serve up not just a filling meal for the body, but a wholesome, nurturing environment where the soul can also be fed.

What can you find at your *grand*parents' home? Food, drink, fellowship, fun, conversation, counsel, encouragement, rest, restoration, advice, perspective, forgiveness, prayers, and hugs and kisses. The light is always on!

What does it mean in practical terms to create a safe haven for your grandchildren? For some, it might include clearing out the basement or a spare bedroom to make room for child-related paraphernalia like games, toys, bicycles, and tricycles. Other families could assign an area in their garage or barn for fun projects for the *grand*parents and grandchildren to do together, such as building a birdhouse, painting a doll house, or planting a vegetable garden. Still other families might set up elaborate swing sets in their backyards or buy cribs and bunk beds for sleep overs.

But let's not limit the term "safe haven" to a merely physical space. By far, the most important type of safe haven is an emotional one—how grandchildren feel when they are with their *grand*parents. If you don't have any space to spare, your safe haven might take the form of a weekly ritual of playing at a nearby park and then chatting over lunch. Or it might entail you bringing a meal to your grandchildren's home to prepare together while their parents go out for a few hours.

*Grand*parents can creatively use the resources they have to make the most of every opportunity to connect with their grandchildren. They do their best not to allow a tight budget, lack of time, or even lack of energy to get in the way of making a safe haven for their grandchildren. They understand that life is too short to squander the chance of meaningfully investing in their grandchildren's lives. *Grand*parents should be honored to have the chance to open their hearts, arms, and homes through words, deeds, sacrifice, and prayer in every season, year after year.

Take-away Action Thought

I will find practical ways to create a safe haven for my grandchildren so they always feel welcomed and loved in my presence.

My Heart's Cry to You, O Lord

Father, please give me fresh and creative ways to create a safe haven for my grandchildren. I want to use everything you've graciously given me. I'm thrilled to share everything I have with my family in a way that will make an eternally lasting difference in my grandchildren's lives. Help me to sensitively weave your love into our conversations so that my grandchildren are confident of our unconditional love for them. Lord, I pray that I would represent you in a way that will awaken in them a desire to enter into an intimate relationship with you. Above all, give me opportunities to pour out that which quenches even the thirstiest soul: your love and peace. May every action taken on my part point them to you, O Lord. Amen.

Grand Ideas

1. Take a good, hard look at the space you have and do what you can to create a specially designated place for your grandchildren where they feel comfortable.
2. This week, carefully plan some new ways to make your grandchildren feel safe and welcomed the next time they visit.
3. If your schedule doesn't allow for special alone time with your grandchildren, invite them to join you in whatever task you're doing, even if their "help" prolongs the job.

Chapter 19

Grandparents Can Help Before/During/After Divorce

The Lord's unfailing love surrounds
the man who trusts in him.

Psalm 32:10

*Trusting God does not mean that we will never have
questions, doubts, or fears. We cannot simply turn off
the natural thoughts and feelings that arise when we
face difficult circumstances. Trusting God means that
in spite of our questions, doubts, and fears we draw
on his grace and continue to believe that he is loving,
that he is in control, and that he is always working for
our good. Such trust helps us to continue doing what
is good and right, even in difficult circumstances.*

Ken Sande

When a close friend's son and daughter-in-law decided to end their seven-year marriage, my friend and her husband stepped in and made a huge difference in the lives of their grandchildren, who were in the frightening no man's land during the divorce. Her life, as well as her husband's retirement years, is not at all what she thought it would be when her son happily announced he and his then wife were expecting their first child five years ago.

Who could have seen this coming? Who would have expected that a once loving daughter-in-law would opt out of both marriage and parenting? No one! But my friend did when her then daughter-in-law began distancing herself from the family and opted out of any parenting responsibility she could. Eventually, the fallout landed directly on her, her husband, and their son. They are now "parenting" the grandchildren the best way they know how. These *grand*parents now care for the grandchildren during the day while their dad is working. Depending on his schedule, sometimes they keep them overnight, getting them up in the morning and taking the oldest to kindergarten—all tasks normally assigned to parents. It's not a surprise that when the youngest grandchild naps midmorning, so do they!

Tough times call for tough measures. My friends never complain because they understand it is through God's mercy that they can support, love, influence, and care for their grandchildren's needs. They also recognize that the emotional trauma of being abandoned by a parent requires them to be, with God's help, a source of healing and restoration to these children. They patiently and faithfully do this one day at a time, one word at a time, and one hug at a time.

What does it look like to make a difference in the lives of grandchildren who have suffered the breakdown of their family? How do *grand*parents help their grandchildren heal from such devastating losses? By bowing their knees before their heavenly Father and asking for wisdom, understanding, and the ways and means to effectively execute their plans.

Next, *grand*parents have conversations with their adult child and ask him or her about their immediate needs. *Grand*parents never overwhelm their adult child by looking too far down the road or anticipating lasting damage to the grandchildren. Rather, they wisely focus on meeting only today's needs. *Grand*parents know that God can transform impossible situations through his enabling grace and power, and they do their best to remind their adult child and grandchildren of this truth. The one thing they never do, though, is assume they know what is best for their grandchildren. *Grand*parents understand that they are meant to take a supportive role, not be the main character, and they maintain a grateful heart to be part of the cast.

Take-away Action Thought

When a great need arises in my family, I will immediately pray for God's wisdom and understanding on the matter. If he so calls me, I will do whatever it takes to patch the family back together and care for my grandchildren.

My Heart's Cry to You, O Lord

Father, our family's heart is breaking over my child's divorce. We never expected this to happen, and we feel shocked and grief-stricken. Please bless us with your abiding strength, a renewal of your daily grace, and the courage to face each day with hope. We remember your promise to never leave or forsake us. Help us communicate that wonderful truth to our adult child and our grandchildren. Work through us to bring healing to our grandchildren and help them transition into this new way of life. Father, you love our family even more than we do, so shower them with your supernatural peace and hope. Amen.

Grand Ideas

1. If divorce becomes part of your adult child's story, make yourself available before/during/after the divorce and help out as much as you can.
2. Even though emotions will be running high, be sure to speak diplomatically and respectfully of your adult child's former spouse.
3. For your own sake, seek godly advice and prayer support from other grandparents who have been down this road before.

 *Chapter 20*

Grandparents Can Temper Life's Losses with Steadfast Love

Do not let your hearts be troubled. You
believe in God; believe also in me.

John 14:1

*When we understand God's sovereignty and submit to his
rule, we can live and speak as God has designed. This
is the polar opposite of living and speaking according
to our plan, for our control, and for our own glory.*

Paul Tripp

*L*oss upon loss. It feels like we face them daily in
today's world. When we read the newspaper, watch
a television newscast, listen to a radio broadcast,
or sit with friends as they share their troubled heart, one
thing is certain: there is no way to get away from or go
around life's losses. Over the past several weeks, our family
received the sad news of six new cancer diagnoses from
close friends. As I've been pondering how to best help them
during their treatments, I must admit my heart is fearful.

Anxious thoughts about more friends being diagnosed with cancer have followed me relentlessly. To try and calm my restless heart and mind, I've been reading all the verses in the Bible about God's sovereignty and trusting in him to provide exactly what we need. One thought, one prayer, that's all I can focus on in the moment of pain. But it's enough. That and asking the Lord for more grace to walk through my own difficulties and support those I love.

*Grand*parents must immediately start preparing themselves for the possibility of difficult tomorrows by reminding themselves of God's promised faithfulness, his unchanging character, and his saving grace. *Grand*parents make themselves strong by reading, studying, meditating, and memorizing key Bible verses that are relevant to both good and bad days. After all, the Bible is powerful, alive, and active, and investing in it is an effective way to prepare for hard times.

I love hearing about *grand*parents who jump into action as soon as someone they love is in a crisis. Whether it's a financial problem, housing dilemma, school situation, scary medical diagnosis, or a relational crisis, they are ready. Impressively, those *grand*parents aren't a fearful, panicky, end-of-the-world kind of ready; they are faithfully secure in God and have emotionally prepared themselves to trust in the Lord no matter what.

*Grand*parents know that when their grandchildren are hurting, their consistent, compassionate, and loving support reminds their grandchildren that they are not alone.

*Grand*parents lead the way through the dark tunnels of despair and fear by offering to pray with and for their grandchildren. And as *grand*parents wisely strengthen their relationship with the Lord in preparation for tragedies, they are examples of how God will provide for their adult child and grandchildren's daily, hourly, and minute-by-minute need for grace.

Take-away Action Thought

When disaster strikes my family, I will offer all the encouragement, hope, and help I can.

My Heart's Cry to You, O Lord

I must look to you first, Lord, when I get word of difficult news. Lift me out of despair when someone I love is in pain, and give me the good sense to turn directly to you for hope and the bigger perspective. I know I cannot control outcomes, answers, or anything, really, so I have to trust you. Give me unshakable faith during my darkest, most feared-filled moments, and then help me pass on that faith to my needful family. Lord, I know that you rule this world and that you sustain us with your power. Help me trust your perfect plan even when I don't understand it. Amen.

Grand Ideas

1. When disaster strikes your family, take every fear you have directly to God. Once you have settled your

own fears and are at peace again, share faith-filled love and encouragement with your family members.

2. Set aside a specific portion of each day to pray about the hardships your family is facing and make a list of Bible verses you can carry with you throughout the day to encourage yourself when you sink into fits of anger or despair.

3. In the event of a catastrophe, ask your friends and church family to pray for you all. Humble yourself and ask for the help you all need instead of keeping people at a distance.

Part Three
How to Become a Grandparent

Chapter 21

Grandparents Take It All to God in Prayer

"We rejoice in our sufferings because we
know that suffering produces perseverance;
perseverance, character, and character, hope.

Romans 5: 3–4

*In our lives God uses conflict not just to make the story
better but to make us better. In life, not just literature, we
repeatedly see that protection from conflict produces soft,
spoiled, and selfish people, while enduring conflict is more
likely to produce someone strong, capable, and caring.*

Randy Alcorn

*I*f I'm honest, I really hate this principle of conflict and
hardship being the tools that God uses to deepen our
faith and strengthen our character. No one enjoys conflict, hardship, or suffering, but I have a unique aversion
to it. However, truth be told my own seasons of suffering
and loss have made me a more effective comforter to others. Although Job's loss of everything he held dear is an
extreme one, there is much to learn from his supernatural,

grace-given, faith-driven response to his pain. First of all, the fact that he got down on the ground and worshipped the Lord in the midst of his horrifying circumstances is absolutely awe-inspiring. Job's example of trust and faithfulness is something worth paying attention to when we face trials (or worse still, when our loved ones face them).

At this writing, I have four adult children and four grandchildren. In addition to my own experiences, I also interviewed women and men for *Empty Nest, What's Next?* and *Preparing, Adjusting, and Loving the Empty Nest.* During this time, I learned a great deal about the regrets parents have from their experience of raising children. Right at the top of these surveys runs one particularly relevant lesson: Not allowing children to feel the consequences of their poor choices keenly enough. Today's *grand*parents recognize the value of allowing pain and some suffering into their grandchildren's lives because they understand that hardship, loss, and personal discomfort nurture strong, giving, selfless, resilient adults. I doubt anyone would refute the idea that those who endured some of the worst experiences life has to offer are often the most giving, mature, kind, and compassionate individuals out there.

One of the more powerful pieces of advice we can give our grandchildren (and our adult children) is the reminder to view every experience (both good and bad) as valuable life lessons, because our character is formed by our reactions to them. Some of the more sensitive *grand*parents might resist accepting this fact, because it requires admitting that loved ones will go through painful circumstances. But in truth, if we shelter our grandchildren from age-appropriate life lessons, we hinder their growth and development as robust children of God.

Wise *grand*parents should welcome the working of God in their grandchildren's lives because of the incredible opportunity for character development, instead of cowering in fear of the temporary discomfort that accompanies difficult circumstances. But this begs the question: What can loving *grand*parents do when a loved one suffers? They get on their knees. They stay on their knees. They pray, pray, pray!

But instead of simply beseeching the Lord for pain relief, ask him to develop strength, patience, kindness, compassion, and resilience in our grandchildren. *Grand*parents liven up their prayer life by beginning and ending their prayers with generous amounts of praise to the Lord by thanking him for completing this good work even before he has begun. Real-life changes can be set into motion only when *grand*parents are on their knees, taking it all to God in prayer.

Take-away Action Thought

When I feel the temptation to alleviate the pain my grandchildren are experiencing, I will pray first and ask the Lord if he is using this difficult time to do something in their lives.

My Heart's Cry to You, O Lord

Father, I truly need your eternal perspective on my grandchildren's lives as they endure pain and suffering. I struggle with the temptation to ease their pain, even though I understand how seasons of suffering help the sufferer grow up and become more sensitive to others' hurt. But because my first response is to alleviate my grandchildren's "seasons of growth," help me to know when and how I can best support them as they learn and grow. Remind me that first and foremost they are yours and that you care for them immeasurably more than I do. Amen.

Grand Ideas

1. When you begin to feel the weight of your grandchildren's suffering, remove yourself (literally) from the situation and get busy praying for God's will to be accomplished in the situation.
2. Include daily intercession for the development of godly character in your grandchildren.
3. If you feel an overwhelming compulsion to alleviate your grandchildren's pain, first take your desires to the Lord and communicate with your adult children. If after both of these steps you are encouraged to be a source of help, then step in and try to help them.

 Chapter 22

Learning from Our Mistakes and Getting It Right as Grandparents

So do not fear, for I am with you; do not be dismayed,
for I am your God. I will strengthen you and help
you; I will uphold you with my righteous right hand.

Isaiah 41:10

*It's really one of the great tasks of your life to
learn how to talk back, and to discover that
these negative tapes are not the voice of God.*

Paula Rinehart

*P*arental mistakes are the tapes that replay in many *grand*parents' minds, causing them to enter into the *grand*parenting arena with trepidation. So many women and men hesitantly share their perceived parental failures, regretful still years after the event. When I hear their painful admissions, I want to shout, "Welcome to the human race!" Every single parent has a litany of failures to our credit. All of us have sin and weaknesses ingrained in the fibers of our hearts, and we all have had our fair share of emotional outbursts, prideful attitudes, and thoughtless comments that wounded the tender souls of our children. Satan gleefully spreads the lie of magnificent proportions that our past failures disqualify us from serving the Lord (and our families). What could be a more effective way to defeat grandparents than by reminding them of their imperfect parenting records?

The wise *grand*parent confesses to the Lord and to their children that they failed. But then, they begin making reparations, learning how to do better, and then doing it. While even *grand*parents of the sturdiest stock will make mistakes in the coming days—and yes, they will have to, at times, ask for forgiveness—they can always move forward. Each step of the parenting and *grand*parenting journey is fraught with potential errors and unintentional missteps. But God, in all his grace, proclaims to us, "Do not fear, for I am with you; do not be dismayed, for I am your God. I will strengthen you and help you; I will uphold you with my righteous right hand" (Isaiah 41:10).

Don't you just love do-overs? I certainly do. I am so grateful that God never gives up on me, despite how slow a learner I am. Truth be told, I'm in awe of the fact that God entrusts helpless babes into the care and keeping of fallible adults. But he did. From the very beginning, he instituted family as the place where we grow, learn, and, yes, make countless mistakes. Family is a beautiful mess worth making.

Even though it may be tempting to obsess about our failings, we must recognize that the Lord has likely protected our children and us from much worse. I wonder how many of my mistakes would have had even greater consequences in my children's lives had God not protected and intervened on their behalf! We must pray every day for the Lord to make up the difference, because we can't be everything our children and grandchildren need. I believe that in spite of our failings, God will answer our cries and make up the difference.

Today, the best we can do is admit our past mistakes, ask for pardon from those we've hurt, and then create a healthier, Bible-focused family from here on out. None of us has any excuse for giving up or giving in to the shame that can paralyze us. Thankfully, God promises to be with us, strengthen us, guide us, and, best of all, uphold us with his righteous right hand.

Take-away Action Thought

When my parental mistakes begin to spin nonstop in my mind and steal my confidence to be an effective *grand*parent, I will read Isaiah 41:10 out loud as many times as needed—until I believe it!

My Heart's Cry to You, O Lord

Please help me to quiet the voices of doubt and fear in my mind. I want to always remember your promise to be with me, strengthen me, and uphold me. Lord, I know that everyone has memories of failing as a parent, but mine frequently come back to haunt me when I see one of my adult children struggling with similar issues. I am paralyzed by their choices even though, as independent adults, I know they must make their own decisions. I'm not afraid of admitting that I've been wrong, and I'm not afraid to ask for forgiveness. But I am afraid of not getting it right with my grandchildren. God, help me to stop focusing on perfection and start serving them in love, in word, and in deed. Amen.

Grand Ideas

1. When memories of past failings swarm you, seek out God's truth through his word and fortify yourself with his promises of forgiveness, grace, and strength.
2. Look back only to learn from your parenting mistakes and, consequentially, work hard to not repeat your past.
3. Seek forgiveness frequently and quickly, and remember that asking for forgiveness will strengthen your relationship with your adult children.

Chapter 23

Repairing Relationships After Past Hurts

Whoever conceals their sins does not prosper, but the
one who confesses and renounces them finds mercy.

Proverbs 28:13

*Godly sorrow will not always be accompanied by
intense feelings, but it implies a change in thinking,
which should lead to changes in behavior.*

Ken Sande

I n the last chapter, we touched on the fact that everyone
makes parenting mistakes. But sometimes these mistakes are severe. In some families, a mother or father
literally abandoned their children. In others, alcohol/drug
abuse caused the parent(s) to neglect and/or abuse their
children. Perhaps a parent emotionally left the family even
though they were physically present, or they engaged in
an extramarital affair that tore the family apart. Some may
have had a gambling or spending problem that brought
the family to their knees financially. The list of serious of-
fences is endless. Looking back over past years of wrongful

behavior, if you believe you owe your adult children more than a simple apology, then you probably do.

Misdemeanor mistakes run along the lines of losing one's temper, feeling irritable and letting everyone know it, ignoring someone when they need your attention, forgetting an important event, treating someone with impatience, talking down to a person—you get the picture. Although these are rather minor, they do have negative effects on other people and the parent's relationship with them. But usually a heartfelt apology and time will heal those wounds.

Conversely, other forms of sin have longer lasting and far more serious repercussions. These sorts of sins are the types listed earlier. In these cases, the parent needs to prayerfully and wisely discern the best way to make reparations, if it's even possible to do so at this point.

In a perfect world, the offenders go to those they hurt, ask for forgiveness for specific instances, and then wait for a hopefully positive reply ("Yes, I forgive you"). After that initial and vital exchange, the relationship can then begin to be healed. The offender has to be willing to listen (humbly and patiently) while the other person tries to verbalize how these actions have impacted their lives. Real forgiveness is the beginning to starting over, but genuine healing can take a lot of time, effort, and commitment. So, be patient once you initiate the process.

I'm often surprised when individuals share their stories from the past with me. In the here and now, these people seem to be doing their level best to be loving

Christ-followers, whole-hearted servants, and intentional *grand*parents. What I don't see is their pain-ridden, mistake-riddled, and damaged past, because their lives have become new in Christ and their faith has dramatically changed them.

Unfortunately, their families experienced living with a very different kind of person and may not be able to see what I now observe. Some families are willing and ready to forgive and give their parent a second chance. Others, maybe not. But regardless, parents who failed in significant ways are faith-bound to seek out forgiveness and then repair the damage, if possible. It doesn't matter which camp your adult children fall into (forgiveness or unforgiveness), you can only do your best to ask for forgiveness. The rest is up to God.

He waits for us to obey, and once we do, he can work wonders. It may take years of patient prayers before our adult children fully forgive us, but in those long, hard seasons of hopeful expectation you can relax in the knowledge that you took the first courageous step and asked for forgiveness, which is all you can do. Only by obeying God will you finally find peace. Seeking forgiveness at this point demonstrates that you truly are a different person. Hopefully, your children will see that you are now worthy of trust and forgiveness and that you can find your place in the family again. Then, as your family watches you thrive in your new, Christ-centered life, God is glorified and lifted up. Finally, as God is glorified, the impossible can happen. Of course, they may never forgive you, but you can rest in the fact that you were honest and vulnerable and expressed the love of Christ wholeheartedly.

℘ Take-away Action Thought

When I am prompted to ask for forgiveness, I will not delay. I will contact my child immediately, ask them to meet with me in person, and humbly apologize.

My Heart's Cry to You, O Lord

Lord, help me to be humble enough to admit when I have inflicted pain on others, and give me the courage to do whatever it takes to restore the relationship. I am truly grief-stricken over the choices I made while they were in my care. I hurt my children and neglected them, and now I am heartbroken over my sin. I want to make it right. Lord, will you prepare the way for me? Will you give me the right words to say, the humility to say it in a way that will soften my child's heart toward me, and the grace to listen to their response? I understand how angry and bitter my children are because of my actions, but I don't want them to be shackled by a lack of forgiveness. Please help them to see my good intentions. Lord, I need your Holy Spirit to bring us together again through reconciliation. I'm placing this in your hands, which is all I can do. Amen.

Grand Ideas

1. When God brings to your mind specific actions you did that have caused your children pain, meet with them as soon as possible so you can humbly ask for their forgiveness.

2. After you have asked for forgiveness, patiently wait for their forgiveness. Don't push them, but pray and trust that God will work in their hearts.

3. Looking back, no doubt you realize you have hurt your family in many ways, and there are some things you cannot repair. However, make a list of areas where you can still offer restitution and do whatever it takes to rebuild a trustful relationship with them.

Chapter 24

Respecting the Parents' Rules and Preferences

Command them to do good, to be rich in good
deeds, and to be generous and willing to share.
1 Timothy 6:18

*The good work of God in our hearts is to free us to
love others without all the costly preoccupation of
having to pose and posture and protect ourselves.*
Paula Rinehart

We might think we always know best, but we don't.
We might believe that our many years of parenting qualify us to tell our now adult children how
to parent their little ones, but they don't. If we persist in
offering unwanted, unwarranted, and unneeded parental
directives, however, we might just forfeit the right to see
our grandchildren. Is forcing our way of doing things onto
someone else worth that? Never. Yet, some grandparents
become irate over the choices their adult children make for
their grandchildren, and as a result, they feel compelled to

apply pressure on these parents. Shockingly, some grandparents try to aggressively overrule their adult children's rules and preferences and even resort to lying (and they urge their grandchildren to lie as well). It's unthinkable!

These misguided grandparents seem to believe that because their adult children have different ideas or ways, they have the right—no, the responsibility!—to override them. This, however, is not the case. If you want to place a wedge in between your adult children and yourself, then go ahead and express every little thought that runs through your brain. Rather than forcing their opinions, *grand*parents need to love without exception and without qualifiers. A real *grand*parent is rich in good deeds, generous, willing to share everything, and cautious to give their opinion on how their grandchildren are being raised.

Underlying the surface-level aspect of honoring our adult children's rules and preferences is the principle of respect. *Grand*parents demonstrate the importance of listening and acquiescing to those whose authority is over them—that is, the parents of their grandchildren. And if you don't believe the grandchildren are watching, watch out! Kids (younger and older) tell their parents everything they see and hear. Endless chatter naturally seems to erupt from at least little ones!

Even if they don't agree, *grand*parents never allow their grandchildren to watch a program the parents have restricted, take grandchildren places they are not allowed to go, or feed them anything not approved by Mom and Dad.

It doesn't matter what the rule-breaking offense might be. Little or large, it's wrong to go against parental decisions. *Grand*parents should have complete trust and confidence in their adult children's rules. They will do nothing, by word or deed, to undermine the respect and authority of Mom and Dad.

Likewise, *grand*parents will seek to instill only positive thoughts and feelings about the parents when they talk about them to their grandchildren. If the grandchildren complain about something their parents have done or said, *grand*parents will do their best to help the children see the situation from their parents' perspective. They will offer supportive words that can ease a tense situation and draw the grandchildren back to their parents. *Grand*parents never indulge in family drama. Rather, they seek to make peace whenever possible. They do so with their words, deeds, and generous hearts.

🕊 *Take-away Action Thought*

When I disagree with my children's choices in parenting my grandchildren, I will not say anything to undermine my adult children in front of others; I will discreetly ask them if we can talk about the issue privately.

My Heart's Cry to You, O Lord

Father, you know that there have been some situations when my children parented my grandchildren differently than I would have done. Help me to let go of the little matters, but also give me opportunities to respectfully discuss larger issues with my grandchildren's parents if I am deeply concerned about something that may hurt or damage the grandchildren. Give me the self-restraint to refrain from overriding the rules or preferences my adult children have set up for their children. Even when I don't see the value or the importance of a specific choice, help me abide by their wishes. In those situations, work through me to demonstrate the importance of respecting those in authority. Bless me with your guiding wisdom to fulfill the grandparenting role and help me to generously love them no matter what. Amen.

Grand Ideas

1. Never undermine your grandchildren's respect for their parents, and do not side with your grandchildren over your adult children.
2. If there are instances when you are truly burdened over a decision your adult children have made for your grandchildren, instead of outright going against them, first ask them to explain their decision.
3. When your grandchildren come to you and complain about their parents' rules and decisions, do your best to explain their parents' perspective.

 Chapter 25

Making Time and Space for Grandchildren

Serve wholeheartedly, as if you were
serving the Lord, not men.

Ephesians 6:7

*The one to whom we pray knows our feelings. He knows
temptation. He has felt discouraged. He has been hungry
and sleepy and tired. . . . He nods in understanding
when we pray in anger. . . . He smiles when we confess
our weariness. . . . He, too, knew the drone of the
humdrum and the weariness that comes with long
days. . . . God became flesh and dwelt among us.*

Max Lucado

Make time and space for what you truly care about. This may mean fitting more fun time with your grandchildren into your week. Or it may entail a larger investment of your time by becoming the designated sitter for several days a week. In some more extreme situations, you may need to take over parenting your grandchildren because your adult child is not fit to do so.

117

Though these scenarios are as varied as the individuals living out their lives, what matters most is the inward attitude of the heart. For example, a friend of mine has taken over the full-time job of parenting her four granddaughters (ages four through ten), making time and space in her home for them. At this date, they have had legal custody for almost two years. My friend hopes and prays that her daughter and son-in-law will get help and eventually regain custody of their daughters. But until then, my friend and her husband have had to make many sacrifices, including their dreams of traveling across the country. Their travel fund is being used instead for food, clothing, medical expenses, haircuts, and the occasional meal out. Are they angry, bitter, or resentful? Not at all. Rather, this older couple is embracing all of life's twists and turns, enjoying this unique, unforeseen opportunity to invest in their granddaughters' lives.

On the flip side, there are people who rarely make time or space for their adult children or grandchildren, despite having been bestowed with an abundance of means to do so. To hear them talk, you wouldn't even know they had any grandchildren at all. Their lives are full of other things: traveling, shopping, salon trips, lunches with friends, and getaways from the stresses of life. Even when gently probed about their families they don't share much information. Worse still to my mind is their assumption that because their children are grown adults, they can now spend their time doing whatever they feel like doing.

How does God desire you to use your time and space to serve your grandchildren and show them the love they need? Perhaps he wants you to schedule a weekly date with them or attend their activities (such as soccer games, school plays, and so on). Maybe he wants you to volunteer to be a helper/aide at your grandchild's school or in your children's ministry at church. Other ideas of ways to be involved include: inviting them over for dinner or dessert, asking them to help you do chores in exchange for some petty cash, doing crafts or games with them, making popcorn, having a bonfire and roasting marshmallows! Of course, a favorite with grandchildren is usually the sleepover at Grandma and Grandpa's. Whatever it may be, find ways to be more involved as much as you are able.

We all need to prioritize our families in such a way that one of the first thoughts we have when we have a bit of "extra" anything is how we can share that with our grandchildren. What is your "extra" this week?

Take-away Action Thought

Each week of the coming year I will prioritize making time and space in my life for my grandchildren.

My Heart's Cry to You, O Lord

Father, I never expected to be as torn between my current responsibilities and having fun with my grandkids. Even though my adult children are out of our home, I still feel as though there are not enough hours in my day. Help me to prioritize how I spend my time wisely. Lord, use your power to illuminate specific days and hours on my calendar I can reserve for my family, and then give me the self-discipline to keep it going all year. I never want to look back over my life and one day realize my grandchildren have grown up without me seeing it happen. Amen.

Grand Ideas

1. This week, talk with your adult children and brainstorm about the most effective ways you can assist them in the coming weeks and months. Together, find the best ways for you to support them throughout their busy lives.
2. Review the next six months and schedule in biweekly or monthly visits with your family.
3. If you feel as though some special circumstances have arisen that place undue pressure on your adult children, offer some of your time to serve your family until the crisis is over.

Chapter 26

Paying Close Attention to How We
Speak to Our Grandchildren

The tongue has the power of life and death,
and those who love it will eat its fruit.

Proverbs 18:21

People hear your words of truth, but
they feel your words of kindness.

Emerson Eggerichs

I can easily tell you about moments when I used my
words rightly to instruct, correct, or discipline my four
children, as well as emphasize God's love and great
purposes for them. However, I can also painfully recall
those times when I said the wrong the thing and hurt my
children. The mystery and power of words demonstrate
that no matter what situation we're in, they can either suc-
ceed marvelously in building someone up or fail pitifully
and crush them. When it comes to our words, we need to
be keenly aware that we can offer life to those who hear
us speak or are on the receiving end of our sentences. It

is so important for us to step back in moments of volatile emotional upheaval to pray, reflect, and then respond. Ultimately, each of us must look at what we want to accomplish in the long run and reconcile that with what comes out of our mouths. When we are instructing, correcting, or even disciplining our grandchildren for their misbehavior, what is it we want most of all? Temporary obedience or long-term character development?

We miss the point if we want our grandchildren to obey us only for the sake of obedience. *Grand*parents need to recognize that their words will either help or harm in rightly nurturing their grandchildren's relationship with the Lord in the long run. With every word we speak, we must impart God's love to our grandchildren and remind them of his purpose for their lives as God reveals it to them over time.

It's not that hard for *grand*parents to pay close attention to their grandchildren. We love to look at their faces, their hands, their toes. *Grand*parents study their grandchildren as if they have never seen a baby before. And we continue to dote on them as they grow and develop. We love our progeny. Aside from the physical development of their grandchildren, *grand*parents also are tuned to the development of their unique personalities and giftedness, and they take every opportunity to point out the positives. *Grand*parents consistently use uplifting words to build confidence and match these affirming statements with real life ways of using their grandchildren's talents to make the world a brighter and better place. They offer suggestions and examples of how their grandchildren too can use their words to encourage others.

Take-away Action Thought

I will pay close attention to my grandchildren whenever I see them, always looking for the best in them. Then, I will affirm those attributes. I will also guard my words, being careful and deliberate in everything I say to them.

My Heart's Cry to You, O Lord

Father, help me to be the type of *grand*parent who seeks only the best for my grandchildren and who nurtures a saving faith in Jesus Christ in them from a young age. Show me how to steer them to you. Give me the words to make a powerful impression upon them of who you are. Even in those moments when my grandchildren are not behaving appropriately, speaking kindly, or evidencing anything positive at all, help me to be gracious, kind, and respectful. Help me to speak to them about your love for them. God, cast a vision on their hearts of how you might use the talents and giftedness you placed within them. Above all, let my words bring joy and peace to their tender hearts and minds. Speak through me, Lord, so that you can accomplish all that you desire. Amen.

Grand Ideas

1. As you spend time talking with your grandchildren, remind yourself to speak only what is helpful to the listener and give your grandchildren the permission to remind you too.

2. If you see something in your grandchild that could grow into a harmful attitude or character trait, step up your prayers for that child, believing that God can and will intervene to keep them on the path toward him.

3. As you spend time with your grandchildren, help them to look for the best in each other. When they start to bicker and squabble, play referee and help guide through a calmer, more civil conversation to work through their differences.

Chapter 27

Teaching Faith, Hope, and Love to Grandchildren

Praise be to the God and Father of our Lord Jesus
Christ, the Father of compassion and the God of
all comfort, who comforts us in all our troubles,
so that we can comfort those in any trouble with
the comfort we ourselves receive from God.

2 Corinthians 1:3–4

*Prayer is vital—but to really experience His
peace, we must come to Him with gratitude. Hard
gratitude. Costly gratitude. The kind that trusts that
He is working for our good even in the unpleasant
circumstances. . . the kind that garrisons our troubled
hearts and minds with His unexplainable peace.*

Nancy Leigh DeMoss

When my good friend's husband died last year
in an automobile accident, it threw their entire
family into an emotional firestorm. This loving
spouse, father, and grandfather was only in his mid-fifties.

At first, everyone was numb because of the shock; the reality of his death hadn't hit yet. After the funeral service, one of their grandchildren asked my friend about a story that had been shared at the service. My friend smiled for the first time in days as she recounted that happy memory to her grandchild. Remembering happy things about her husband and what they had shared together was a good start to her grieving process. Telling stories about him prolongs his legacy and keeps the memory of him alive, so much so that his incredible example of faith will continue to bless his grandchildren.

Not everyone will be faced with the unexpected loss of a spouse in such a dramatic and sudden way. Some may receive a cancer diagnosis that may not claim their life but greatly diminish it. Others will lose jobs, finances, homes, friends, health, or even mental stability. No matter what form our suffering takes, we must stand strong in our belief that God is with us in our pain and that he is working for our good in the midst of even the most traumatic circumstances. Our grandchildren will be watching to see how we respond to life's curve balls. Will we turn away from God in anger and bitterness when tragedy strikes? Or will we choose to lean into Jesus during our darkest moments, thereby offering our grandchildren an example of what it means to follow Christ even during seasons of suffering? *Grand*parents choose faith, hope, and love. They choose it for themselves and for their grandchildren.

Faith, hope, and love. Faith, in our unchanging God, who is always working for our good and his glory. Hope, that no matter how dark the situation may seem, God is still reigning righteously over all of it. Love, the golden thread that runs through every person's life, believing that God will have the last word in every circumstance. Faith, hope, and love. *Grand*parents must intentionally nurture these three Christian attributes in their own lives. They do it for themselves so as to be fully equipped for the dark days that come to all of us. They also do it to hold out the light of Jesus Christ—the light that is never extinguished—for their children and grandchildren to see.

Our grandchildren will see these three biblical light posts shining the way toward Jesus in the midst of hard times, good times, and all the times in between. *Grand*parents hunker down in the depths of God's unfailing love every day so that when others are drowning in sorrow, they can reach out and offer renewed faith, hope, and love. Yes, *grand*parents hurt just like everyone else, but the longer they walk with the Lord, the more they come to understand that all they really need is him. As they get older, *grand*parents see and experience an increase of every type of loss, but in equal measure they know the comfort of God.

🎗 *Take-away Action Thought*

When terrible suffering hits our family, I will comfort myself and my grandchildren by standing firm on the faith, hope, and love of God.

My Heart's Cry to You, O Lord

Help me, Father, to keep my eyes on you during life's painful seasons. I realize that loss is common to humanity and that only you offer the comfort I need to make it through. Remind me of your constant love for me and my grandchildren. Help me to speak words laced with faith, hope, and love to my grandchildren so that they run directly to you for comfort. Give me the strength I need to process my own grief, and then show me how to comfort those I love. Only you can bring hope and healing to a broken heart. Only you can rescue those who are dying—both literally and figuratively. Send your Holy Spirit to save, to heal, and to comfort. Also, give me a grateful heart, so that my trust in you will never waver. Amen.

Grand Ideas

1. *Faith.* When you are in the midst of an unthinkable storm of life, cling to your faith even when your emotions are upended. Share your faith with your grandchildren by reminding them of verses in the Bible that proclaim God's promise to protect and provide for them.

2. *Hope.* When you are weary with grief and struggling to take the next step, nurture your hope in God through prayer and meditation. Look for verses that speak of hope and share them with your grandchildren.

3. *Love.* Even during seasons when you don't feel loved or when it is difficult to love others, commit 1 Corinthians 13 to memory. Then use it as a guideline for your behavior in all circumstances to be an example for your grandchildren.

Chapter 28

Making Priceless Memories

There is . . . a time to weep and a time to laugh.
Ecclesiastes 3:1, 4

*There is no more consistent, pregnant, dynamic
forum for instruction about life than the family,
because that is exactly what God designed
the family to be, a learning community.*

Paul Tripp

After the miscarriage of her daughter's third baby, Jenn believed her entire family needed a break from the sorrow. Certainly it is right and appropriate to spend time grieving and then healing from such a loss. But Jenn knew something else. Because of her many experiences with loss, Jenn knew that laughter can heal broken hearts and wounded spirits. Of course, Jenn wasn't trying to short-circuit her daughter's pain. She was, however, trying to coax smiles back onto her family's faces. Jenn knew what her daughter, son-in-law, and grandchildren loved most of all: splashing in the ocean, basking in the sun, and walking along sandy beaches. So she rented a home near the beach for a week, letting the ocean, sun, and sand do the heavy lifting of helping her family begin to heal.

Jenn, like so many *grand*parents, suffers right along with her adult children and her grandchildren. If the family hurts, so do the *grand*parents. Jenn prayed nonstop for her daughter, her son-in-law, and their two children. While she knew that only God heals the deepest recesses of a broken heart, Jenn also understood the power of even the smallest gesture of kindness from loved ones along the way to recovery. Jenn was determined to keep offering subtle, positive, encouraging, and lighthearted reminders that even after a horrible loss we can learn to laugh again. Jenn, with her kindhearted ways and careful planning, created a priceless memory for her family that week at the seashore. It was one they never forgot and often refer to with wistful, happy faces. Mission accomplished.

Family. A learning community. Don't you love that definition from Paul Tripp? I sure do. That description brings memories of my husband teaching our grandchildren to work on a car, labor in the garden, or tear out dead trees in our woods out back. I also picture myself in the kitchen, rolling out homemade pizza dough or cinnamon rolls while my granddaughter (hands covered in flour) helps at my side. Life is all about learning. We are never too old to tackle a new task, practice a different skill, and then teach our grandchildren what we've learned.

Enjoyable as it is to spend time teaching our grandchildren practical life skills, I believe there is another type of teaching that makes an even bigger impact. *Grand*parents should seize the ordinary moments in life and transform them into priceless memories with intention and planning. *Grand*parents realize that they don't need to spend thousands of dollars (which they may or may not have) to create priceless memories. *Grand*parents seize the moment by working side by side with their grandchildren in even the most seemingly mundane settings—garages, gardens, kitchens—because you can be anywhere to talk about the things that matters most: that is, the wonderful ways God has worked in their lives and will continue to be with them. Grandchildren look up to, listen to, and learn from *grand*parents, regardless of the setting. Make a priceless memory today. Don't waste a moment.

Take-away Action Thought

I will intentionally turn ordinary moments into priceless memories every time I'm with my grandchildren.

My Heart's Cry to You, O Lord

Open my eyes, Father, to see the eternal in the mundane moments of my life. Show me how to use every opportunity to speak to my grandchildren about you and your love, faithfulness, goodness, and grace. Help me breathe life into your truth when I talk about it with my family. Remind me of specific moments when you rescued and strengthened me. Help me to bring laughter to my family. I know that we must grieve our losses, but I also know that you want us to smile, laugh, and have fun. Show me how to integrate lightheartedness and laughter into conversation when it is appropriate. Life is hard and loss comes to us all. But you, Lord, give and give and give whatever it is we need: strength, grace, hope, forgiveness, and love. May my words demonstrate these truths to my grandchildren. Let none of us get bogged down in our sadness and grief. Rather, continually guide us toward healing, joy, and even laughter. Amen.

Grand Ideas

1. When your family suffers a devastating loss, look for creative ways to lighten their grief with precious family time, love, and laughter.
2. Don't simply view time with your grandchildren as "babysitting." Instead, see these hours as perfect opportunities to create priceless, lifetime memories.
3. During those visits when you have tasks to do, intentionally include your grandchildren, going slowly enough to teach them life skills and create wonderful memories.

Chapter 29

Sacrificing for Grandchildren

It is God who arms me with strength
and keeps my way secure.
Psalm 18:32

*You can't go back and make a new start, but you can
start right now and make a brand new ending.*
James R. Sherman

couple I know used to be big spenders. Credit
cards maxed out. No savings. Living paycheck to
paycheck for years. They knew it wasn't healthy,
wise, or in any way honoring to God to be so irresponsible
with their funds, but neither did they make much attempt
to reign in their spendthrift ways. As they neared retirement, this couple met with a financial advisor who pretty
much threw their entire plan for a loop. Using the facts
and showing them their numbers, he warned them that
they would never be able to consider retiring unless they
dramatically changed their spending habits. They left the
meeting feeling shaken and shattered. Both the husband

and the wife had counted on retirement funds that had shrunk, and neither had figured in the rising cost of health insurance premiums among other life necessities. Once the initial shock wore off, they scheduled another sit-down with their advisor, and he gave them the baby-steps of learning to be financially responsible.

In black and white, this couple learned how to alter the way they viewed money. The financial advisor offered them a difficult plan to follow, but it was one that would yield financial freedom over time. Would it result in the wealth of their dreams? No. But if they followed through with his recommendations, this couple could eventually realize their goal of retirement with a modest residual income to sustain them. Of course, they spent more time reflecting on how their foolhardy spending was costing them today and their long tomorrows. What saddened them most was that they were accustomed to spending wild amounts of money on their grandchildren, and unfortunately that extravagance had to come to a swift halt. Sacrifice was about to become their daily reality, as well as a hardship that would impact their adult children and grandchildren.

Hopefully the majority of grandparents won't be forced to reexamine their lifestyle habits and spending in such a dramatic way as the couple described above. It's sad that neither of these two adults stopped long enough to see into their future, simply because they were too busy trying to fulfill whatever whim caught their attention at the moment. Although it is painful to receive such a difficult wake-up call, they are now pursuing a debt-free lifestyle and have become quite vocal about warning others to avoid their mistakes. This couple is learning firsthand what personal sacrifice looks like from a financial perspective.

Then, there are the other *grand*parents who happily put a little aside for their grandchildren whenever extra funds come their way. They are already looking ahead to when their grandchildren may want to attend college, enroll in a vocational school, start a business, or be part of a mission trip. These *grand*parents remember how scarce money was during their young adult years and are eager to help offset some of the cost and partner with their grandchildren's endeavors. *Grand*parents also squirrel away money month to month, year to year, so that they can pamper the family with a special experience, like going out to a nice meal or a vacation. They understand that raising children is expensive, so they are happy to share their abundance with their family. *Grand*parents also realize that making sacrifices develops character, making them more like Christ. Sacrifice begins in the heart of *grand*parents who can envision the positive effects of their investments (whether those investments be time, talents, gifts of service, or monetary in nature) in the lives of their grandchildren.

Take-away Action Thought

I will examine my budget closely and find a way to consistently save so that I can help make my grandchildren's dreams come true.

My Heart's Cry to You, O Lord

Finances are always a delicate subject in our family, Lord. Too often we simply say we cannot afford helping our grandchildren save for college, go on a trip, or even fulfill one of their dreams. This shouldn't be so. Your word tells us that everything in the world is yours, and I should treat my money as such. God, help me to discipline my spending so I am able to support the goals and dreams of my grandchildren. I know that even the smallest amounts of money can grow into a tidy sum when set aside over long periods of time. Help me to make a plan and then stick to it. Give me the wisdom and opportunities to stretch our money so that we can set aside more and more with each passing year. Simplify our needs and wants so that we can broaden our grandchildren's life experiences. Amen.

Grand Ideas

1. Begin setting aside a small portion of your monthly income so you will have the blessing of giving your grandchildren a sum of money for college or some other worthy goal if you are able.
2. Looking over your monthly budget, find areas where you're spending too much money and can cut back. Whatever extra money you accumulate, put toward a special family outing, a nice dinner out, or a mini-vacation.
3. In order to live debt-free, use your credit cards only if you are able to pay it off completely every month.

Chapter 30

Leading Grandchildren to Faith in Jesus Christ

He decreed statutes for Jacob and established the law in Israel, which he commanded our ancestors to teach their children, so the next generation would know them, even the children yet to be born, and they in turn would tell their children. Then they would put their trust in God and would not forget his deeds but would keep his commands.

Psalm 78:5–7

God does not give us overcoming life—He gives us life and we overcome. The strain of life is what builds our strength. If there is no strain, there will be no strength.

Oswald Chambers

I have several heroes in this life. I think about how each of them is currently facing some of the hardest, most pain-ridden challenges, yet they continue to maintain a buoyant, winsome, and happy spirit. While they are fighting completely unique battles, they all have one thing in common: These people have purposed to never give up or give in to depression, despair, or defeat.

One of these heroes of mine is parenting her brood of grandchildren with no end in sight. Another hero is caring for her elderly and infirm parents while also offering daily support to her adult son who is battling cancer. Yet another hero is suddenly single after her spouse died unexpectedly, but she still continues to offer care to her adult daughter's children. These valiant women, who is each dealing with unique and paralyzing challenges, are among the most grateful, humble, and gracious individuals I've ever known. I watch their lives with admiration. When I imagine myself in their position, I wonder if I would fare as well.

Aside from dealing with their daily trials, my heroes are most concerned about their grandchildren's spiritual well-being. Each of these women is, in every sense of the word, the ultimate *grand*mother. Through words and actions, they demonstrate how valued their grandchildren are. They intentionally pray for God to intervene in their grandchildren's lives at a young and tender age. They support their adult children's efforts to create a biblically sound community for their grandchildren. My heroes don't understand the word *impossible* because they know what a great, powerful, and awesome God we love and serve.

*Grand*parents take seriously the biblical mandate from Psalm 78:5–7. They make it their life's mission to see their adult children, grandchildren, and, God willing, their great-grandchildren come to a saving faith in Jesus Christ. They aim to use every opportunity to draw their grandchildren to Jesus. They understand that this life is quickly passing away and that only God's word and human souls last forever. They pray day and night for their grandchildren, proclaiming God's promises out loud as well as silently while meditating. They serve selflessly in both large and small ways. They pay close attention to their grandchildren's unique needs and meet them if possible. They speak affirming words of faith, hope, and love. They never, ever give up. To their dying breath, *grand*parents keep their eyes trained on the Lord with the confidence that he will follow through and draw all their grandchildren under his comforting wings.

Take-away Action Thought

I will make it a daily habit to intercede for my grandchildren's salvation. Even when they're stubborn and unwilling to open their hearts, I will never give up.

My Heart's Cry to You, O Lord

Father, help me to always keep my heart and mind on you. Give me the strength, stamina, and will to continue to pray for my grandchildren. Lord, I long to see them, every one, come at a young age to a saving faith in you. I want them to avoid the pain I experienced as a young person who didn't know you personally. No matter what may happen in their lives, give me the faith, hope, and love to pray with boldness. I refuse to believe that anything is impossible because I know you. I trust in your power and ability to draw my grandchildren to Jesus. I want to remind them of all you have done, and as I do so, I am also reminding myself and strengthening my own faith. Help me to stay focused as I intercede. I believe with all my heart that you are working in their hearts every hour of every day. Amen.

Grand Ideas

1. No matter what obstacles you face in life, embrace an eternal perspective and place your trust in God's faithfulness to carry you through. Gently share your faith with your grandchildren with every opportunity.
2. Prayerfully seek the best moments to share your faith in Jesus Christ with your grandchildren. Obey the nudges of the Holy Spirit and rely on God's ability to give you exactly the right words to say to them at just the right time.
3. Never stop interceding for your adult children or your grandchildren. Even when your heart is broken over the choices they may make in life, continue to put all of your trust and faith in God's ability to radically turn their lives around. Doubt should have no place in your heart or your mind.

Sources for Quotations

1. Paul David Tripp, *Age of Opportunity* (Phillipsburg, NJ: P & R Publishing, 2001), 115.

2. "Grand" definition from https://www.merriam-webster.com.

3. Oswald Chambers, *My Utmost for His Highest* (Grand Rapids: Discovery House, 1992), October 17 entry.

4. Paul David Tripp, *Instruments in the Redeemer's Hands* (Phillipsburg, NJ: P & R Publishing, 2002), 275.

5. Nancy Leigh DeMoss, *Choosing Gratitude* (Chicago: Moody Publishers, 2009), 92–93.

6. Tim Lane and Paul David Tripp, *Relationships: A Mess Worth Making* (Glenside, PA: New Growth Press, 2006), 74–75.

7. Randy Alcorn, *90 Days of God's Goodness* (Colorado Springs: Multnomah, 2011), 111.

8. Max Lucado, *Everyday Blessings* (Nashville: Thomas Nelson, 2004), 127.

9. Lucado, *Everyday Blessings*, 40.

10. Alcorn, *90 Days of God's Goodness*, 236–37.

11. Jennie Allen, *Nothing to Prove* (New York, NY: WaterBrook, 2017), 131.

12. Tripp, *Age of Opportunity*, 158.

13. Tripp, *Instruments in the Redeemer's Hands*, 284.

14. Emerson Eggerichs, *Before You Hit Send* (Nashville: W Publishing Group, 2017), 108–09.

15. Heidi St. John, *Becoming Mom Strong* (Carol Stream, IL: Tyndale, 2017), 74.

16. C. S. Lewis, in Lane and Tripp, *Relationships*, 93.

17. Alcorn, *90 Days of God's Goodness*, 173.

18. Lucado, *Everyday Blessings*, 49.

19. Ken Sande, *The Peacemaker* (Grand Rapids: Baker Books, 2004), 65.

20. Paul David Tripp, War of Words (Phillipsburg, NJ: P & R Publishing, 2000), 69.

21. Alcorn, *90 Days of God's Goodness*, 5.

22. Paula Rinehart, *Strong Women, Soft Hearts* (Nashville: Thomas Nelson, 2001), 164.

23. Sande, *The Peacemaker*, 119.

24. Rinehart, *Strong Women, Soft Hearts*, 144.

25. Lucado, *Everyday Blessings*, 80.

26. Eggerichs, *Before You Hit Send*, 63.

27. DeMoss, *Choosing Gratitude*, 66.

28. Tripp, *Age of Opportunity*, 42.

29. James R. Sherman, *Rejection: How to Survive Rejection and Promote Acceptance* (Golden Valley, MN: Pathway Books, 1982), 45.

30. Chambers, *My Utmost for His Highest*, August 2 entry.